"Men beware; *Boys of a Feather* will pluck away your most intimate courting secrets. Women rejoice; this handy dating guide will provide the insight you need to make your romantic life fly. A very funny book."
　　—Robert Lanham
　　　　Author of *The Hipster Handbook*

"*Boys of a Feather* offers hysterical comparisons that will have you nodding your head with a knowing smirk ... and forever after obsessing over spotting and identifying North American Males in the urban wilds."
　　—Julia Bourland
　　　　Author of *The Go-Girl Guide:*
　　　　Surviving Your 20s with Savvy, Soul, and Style

"A surprisingly astute and hilarious typology of the male species, *Boys of a Feather* should be required reading for all single birds!"
　　—Lucinda Rosenfeld,
　　　　author of *What She Saw* ... and
　　　　Why She Went Home

Boys of a Feather

A FIELD GUIDE TO NORTH AMERICAN MALES

Amy Helmes and Meg Leder
Illustrations by Scott Thigpen

A Perigee Book

THE BERKLEY PUBLISHING GROUP
Published by the Penguin Group
Penguin Group (USA) Inc.
375 Hudson Street, New York, New York 10014, USA
Penguin Group (Canada), 10 Alcorn Avenue, Toronto, Ontario, M4V 3B2, Canada
(a division of Pearson Penguin Canada Inc.)
Penguin Books Ltd., 80 Strand, London WC2R 0RL, England
Penguin Group Ireland, 25 St. Stephen's Green, Dublin 2, Ireland (a division of Penguin Books Ltd.)
Penguin Group (Australia), 250 Camberwell Road, Camberwell, Victoria 3124, Australia
(a division of Pearson Australia Group Pty. Ltd.)
Penguin Books India Pvt. Ltd., 11 Community Centre, Panchsheel Park, New Delhi—110 017, India
Penguin Books (NZ), cnr. Airborne and Rosedale Roads, Albany, Auckland 1310, New Zealand
(a division of Pearson New Zealand Ltd.)
Penguin Books (South Africa) (Pty.) Ltd., 24 Sturdee Avenue, Rosebank, Johannesburg 2196,
South Africa
Penguin Books Ltd., Registered Offices: 80 Strand, London WC2R 0RL, England

Copyright © 2005 by Amy Helmes and Meg Leder
Text design by Tiffany Estreicher
Cover design and art by Scott Thigpen

PRINTING HISTORY
Perigee trade paperback edition / June 2005

PERIGEE is a registered trademark of Penguin Group (USA) Inc.
The "P" design is a trademark belonging to Penguin Group (USA) Inc.

Library of Congress Cataloging-in-Publication Information

Helmes, Amy.
  Boys of a feather : a field guide to North American males / by Amy Helmes and Meg Leder.
      p. cm.
  ISBN 0-399-53154-8
  1. Men—North America—Humor.   I. Leder, Meg, 1974–   II. Title.

PN6231.M45H45   2004
818'.5404—dc22

                                                                          2004043163

PRINTED IN THE UNITED STATES OF AMERICA

10   9   8   7   6   5   4   3   2   1

Most Perigee Books are available at special quantity discounts for bulk purchases
for sales promotions, premiums, fund-raising or educational use. Special books,
or book excerpts, can also be created to fit specific needs.

For details, write: Special Markets, The Berkley Publishing Group, 375 Hudson
Street, New York, New York 10014.

Acknowledgments

The authors would like to thank:

Our agent extraordinaire, Elisabeth Weed, for laughing out loud (in a good way) at our writing and for always watching our back.

Our lovely editor, Michelle Howry, for shaping and refining our research in the most brillant and smart way.

Our savvy illustrator, Scott Thigpen, for bringing our "specimens" to life with enthusiasm.

Our moms, Phyllis and Pat, for teaching us how to avoid Vultures, and our dads, Jack and Jim, equal parts Turkey and Eagle.

Our friends, whose dating highlight reels and horror stories helped inspire this work, and whose support makes bad days good.

And finally, to all the boys who made us fall madly in love or fall badly out of it—thanks for making it all possible.

Introduction

Whether you're exploring city streets, wandering windswept plains, venturing along coastal lowlands, or climbing craggy mountain bluffs, chances are you've encountered one of Mother Nature's most abundant, yet cryptic, creatures. Many congregate in flocks or migrate to the far reaches of our great planet. Still others fly solo, building permanent nests in their quest to mate for life. Glimpsing one in the wild can evoke unspeakable delight. Yet due in part to their perplexing behavioral diversity and an uncanny ability to take flight when you least expect it, these creatures remain something of a mystery.

We're referring to the human male, of course. With an unfathomable spectrum of species, from the near extinct Pegs-His-Pants Boy to the lofty No-TV Guy, understanding this vast anthropological assortment can be baffling and intimidating for even the most intrepid boywatcher.

With that in mind, this illustrated reference tool

offers a male classification system derived from countless hours of observation, interviews, and fieldwork. If you're on the hunt for a potential mate or are interested in boys merely as hobby, *Boys of a Feather* will provide you with tools for understanding and even predicting the behavior of guys who fly across your path.

Consider the rare and elusive Eagle (think J. F. K. Jr.). While millions of single women would sell their soul (or even worse, face reality-TV humiliation) to land such a prized breed, many don't have a clue where to find him in the wild. (Hint: He ain't at Hooters.) This guide will equip you with the know-how and wherewithal to locate and lure the man of your dreams, whether he's a pleasant Parakeet or a swooning, sentimental Lovebird.

By the same token, your fieldwork may bring you into contact with a few "bad eggs." Like those screeching beaked bullies in Hitchcock's *The Birds*, some men have a malicious streak (though they usually skip the eye-gouging and go straight for the heart). Other boy breeds aren't so much cruel as cluelessly sweet and insubstantial—like a marshmallow Peep. *Boys of a Feather* provides you with the cautionary clues to let you avoid the breeds that will break your spirit or simply bore you to tears.

In this book, you'll find a key classification system to guide you in your endeavors:

PLUMAGE: Often the first and easiest way to identify a particular breed, physical appearance provides a general indication of what a boy is all about. Indeed, clothing can and does make the man—along with grooming habits, stature, facial expressions, and the like.

BEHAVIOR: How a particular species operates in the wild is a key indicator of what makes him tick. This category spells out a boy's innate habits and instincts, and why they make him unique.

MATING HABITS: Of particular interest, this category describes how said boy responds around members of the opposite sex. Rituals of courtship, romance, and breeding are all addressed.

HABITAT: Boys of a feather supposedly flock together, but where? This category clues in boywatchers on the public places and geographical locales their subjects are likely to frequent.

NEST: Whether it's a veritable castle or a bundle of sticks with a few IKEA furnishings, a man's home can help you decipher more about his lifestyle. We'll tell you what to look for when scouting out the domicile.

HOW TO LURE: To attract a particular species, you're going to need some breadcrumbs, metaphorically speaking. Every boy demands a slightly different tack, and this section provides surefire methods to train his eyes on you.

FEATURES OF FLIGHT: Considering that boys are a fleeting bunch, this category offers cautionary advice on how, when, and why your species might fly the coop.

PRIZED FOR: While you may never find the goose that laid the golden egg, rest assured that every guy out there has a quality worth treasuring. You just need to figure out what it is, and this portion of *Boys of a Feather* does just that.

Much as Charles Darwin suffered public scorn for his insights on the origin of man, we expect this field guide to be somewhat provocative. In categorizing a variety of specimens, we are in no way attempting to label, malign, or pigeonhole those who sport the XY chromosome. Indeed, one woman's Turkey may be another woman's bird of paradise. And while most scientific endeavors require an adherence to logic and reason over emotion, it's damn near impossible to separate passion from polemics in this line of work. Suffice to say, our system (though not flawless) is a thorough attempt to objectively produce order from chaos, reason from madness, hilarity from hellish dates.

We hope this book will be a handy resource for referencing the men in your life and perhaps make the dating experience just a bit more tolerable (or at least laughable). Sure, it may require lots of patience and painstaking fieldwork, but once you've spotted that breathtaking specimen perched at the corner Starbucks or standing in line at the DMV, you'll be happy you have this handy guide book to inform your next move. (Presumably, you'll elect to ditch the cumbersome binoculars, safari hat, and hideous khaki vest—really, there's no need to sacrifice fashion in the name of research.)

Good luck, and happy hunting!

Check-me-out pout

Body toned with help from personal trainer, Serge

Tailored-to-fit garb from Hugo, Calvin, Ralph, and Co.

Keys to limited-edition luxury sports car

1

Peacocks

I see a man who has serious intentions, that's Levin; and I see a peacock, like this featherhead, who's only amusing himself.

—Leo Tolstoy, *Anna Karenina*

Remember that the most beautiful things in the world are the most useless; peacocks and lilies for instance.

—John Ruskin, *The Stones of Venice*

You've seen them at zoos, strutting about proudly—a gorgeous display of color and show and in-your-face masculinity. In the bird world, peacocks make their presence known with lots of flashy pomp and circumstance, and the same holds true for this family of men. Having a near-obsessive concern for appearance, a penchant for material excess, and an attitude that screams "Look at me!" it's never hard to spot a Peacock in public. Simply keep an eye out for the guy flaunting his proverbial tail feathers.

PLUMAGE: Just as a true peacock causes a scene with his dazzling fantail of spotted iridescence, the Peacock boy is forever the center of attention, puffing out his chest to show off high-priced threads and self-proclaimed "murderous" good looks. Peacocks use costly amounts of product to achieve a glistening, mussed look. They're also frequent molters, shedding last week's Hugo Boss shirt for this week's Armani sweater—all on a body you could bounce a quarter off. If a picture of a Peacock could say a thousand words, he'd stick to just eight: "Brace yourselves, ladies: I am *indeed* this handsome!"

BEHAVIOR: Suffice it to say, humility is not the Peacock boy's strong suit. He is often mesmerized by mirrors, losing himself in a trancelike state as he admires his appearance. In fact, shiny objects of any sort tend to capture his attention, be it gold bullion or the chrome bumper of the sparkling candy-apple red Maserati parked in his driveway.

MATING HABITS: As the number one love in his life is ultimately himself, a Peacock boy prefers women who look good hanging off his arm and who validate his sense of importance. If he's not dating a model, at the very least, he'll gravitate to someone who can worship his beauty and stroke his ego.

HABITAT: Peacocks shine among the unwashed masses at the town's priciest restaurants, concerts (box seats), and nightclubs and make conscious efforts to perpetually be everyone's center of attention, arriving at parties late and stealing the mic to make toasts at a second-cousin's wedding. They're rarely, if ever, found in secluded environments, such as wooded habitats, houses of worship, or musty used bookstores.

NEST: Largely an urban dweller, the Peacock is drawn to high-rise penthouses and trendy neighborhoods. Expect a nest as fabulously attended to as his plumage: upscale Eames chairs and Alessi kitchenware, city skyline views, high-tech light fixtures, and a minimalist decorative scheme (black, stainless steel, white).

HOW TO LURE: Peacocks live to be admired, so you'll have to set yourself apart from his crowd of groupies in order to land him. Present yourself as that elusive Helen of Troy—the gorgeous goddess every male admires (and every female hates)—and he'll be sending a drink your way in under five minutes. From there, simply admire him, treat him as if he's famous, and you'll win his heart, or at least be deemed worthy enough to hang out with him.

FLIGHT PATTERN: Don't even think about shearing your lovely tresses, dressing down in sweat suits, getting a breast reduction, or adding an ounce of fat. If you do, he'll tell you, "You've let yourself go," and then he'll promptly let *you* go.

PRIZED FOR: Whether he has a million bucks or just looks it, the Peacock can prompt awe from onlookers without uttering a single word. He's living in a material world, but if you're his material girl, you'll certainly reap many benefits.

Subspecies

The Fashionista
(Versaci narcissus)

From Gucci sunglasses to Prada man bags, the Fashionista exhibits a superior fashion sense, possessing an uncanny ability to spend large amounts of money on clothes without going broke, even when it seems logically beyond his means. However sleek he appears while modeling the new "it" designer's wares, be forewarned that his style can occasionally go awry—à la Carrie Bradshaw—when he tries something a bit too avant-garde, like wearing a kilt with moon boots.

BOY TIP: To lure a Fashionista, prime yourself to be the perfect accessory: Wear name brand labels. Acquire a chic haircut. Your chances improve dramatically if you resemble Heidi Klum or the late Caroline Bessette Kennedy. Just beware: The instinctual nature of the species doesn't allow for much long-term commitment as long term = dated = unfashionable.

CHARACTERISTIC SONG: "Fashion" by David Bowie; "Sharp Dressed Man" by ZZ Top.

The Dough Boy
(Cashius collectivus)

Spends money, talks money, makes money, ponders ways to make more money. As the Dough Boy prefers to date exclusively within his species, he'll subtly feel out your financial situation with loaded questions: "Oh that *Seabiscuit* . . . great film. I grew up playing polo. Do you ride?" He has more plastic than a Tupperware lady and has been known to whip out a C-note to pay for a pack of Altoids.

BOY TIP: As the Dough Boy is highly wrapped up in his fiscal success, it is difficult to lure him out of his work environment. A healthy dose of naïve appreciation (real or feigned) for his financial prowess helps.

CHARACTERISTIC SONG: "Money" by Pink Floyd; "I Wanna Be Rich" by Calloway.

I Love My Car Guy
(*The autoeroticus*)

Deviating from other Peacocks, I Love My Car Guy is more concerned with his car's appearance than with his own, and spends excessive time "parking": lovingly stroking, washing, and oooh . . . waxing his vehicle. When he does go out, he makes extreme efforts to park said vehicle in the nether regions of public lots, and on return, he'll investigate every microscopic mark on the car's surface, asking, "Was that there before?"

BOY TIP: When interacting with I Love My Car Guy, it's helpful to learn some automotive lingo to bandy about, preferably suggestive terms like "forward drive shaft." Remember to appreciate and respect the car—it is, in essence, the symbolic mother—the first woman in his life.

CHARACTERISTIC SONG: Wilson Pickett's "Mustang Sally"; but *not* "Baby You Can Drive My Car," by the Beatles, as he doesn't agree with the message of the song.

Hatchling Behavior

As a child, the Peacock compulsively hoarded his milk money and allowance, saving up for Matchbox cars or the hottest new pair of Underoos, or simply saving for the satisfaction of having an almost-full piggy bank.

Peacocks

and the Women Who Love Them . . .

If you're looking for a Prince Charming with bucks, then Peacocks are your birds of paradise. You believe having a boyfriend with style and panache (or at least a smokin' ride) is an important accessory—nearly as crucial as having the right handbag and matching jewelry. After all, first impressions say a lot, and sometimes you *really can* judge a book by its cover. Money, power, and good looks may not be the most vital things in life, but you certainly know that a few greenbacks, the right connections, and a pretty face can make life a lot more enjoyable. Sure, you can't take it with you, but why not take it while you can get it?

Ratty hat from frat days of yore

Ill-considered Celtic tattoo courtesy of Spring Break '96

Abdominal subcutaneous cellulite (aka, beer belly)

Wild Turkey

2

Turkeys

A turkey is more occult and awful than all the angels and archangels. Insofar as God has partly revealed to us an angelic world, he has partly told us what an angel means. But God has never told us what a turkey means. And if you go and stare at a live turkey for an hour or two, you will find by the end of it that the enigma has rather increased than diminished.

    —Gilbert Keith Chesterton, *All Things Considered*

We recommend that no one eat more than two tons of turkey—that's what it would take to poison someone.

    —Elizabeth Whelan, *US News & World Report*

While turkeys may be undeserving of all the intellectual scorn heaped upon them, it's still safe to say they aren't the Einsteins of the bird world. Even centuries ago, they were perceived as dim and foolish—some Native American tribes wouldn't eat turkey for fear the bird's stupidity would dull their warlike prowess. Their rep hasn't improved in recent years. Domestic turkeys have been observed looking upward in the sky during rainstorms—reasons unknown—only to drown when their nostrils fill with too much water. Much like their bird counterparts, Turkey boys frequently engage in cryptic and foolish behavior that confounds even the most free-spirited and wacky among us. Metaphorically speaking, they, too, stare at stormy skies, though to the outside observer, it appears they don't have enough sense to come in from the rain.

PLUMAGE: Just as real-life turkeys are easily identified by their strange and unattractive wattle, Turkey boys are distinguished by their inability to determine when a look is ridiculous and inappropriate for the situation at hand, whether it's wearing a Looney Tunes tie at a funeral, an unbuttoned shirt (sans undershirt and with hairy chest) at the office, or a fanny pack *anywhere*.

BEHAVIOR: To put it mildly, Turkeys just don't get it. While his behavior would be appropriate if he were Jim Carrey or a character on a bad television sitcom, in the everyday world his antics go over like a ten-pound frozen Butterball falling out of a fourth-story window. Indeed, the Turkey's attempts at normalcy always fall flat thanks to his bizarre impulse to openly pick his nose or his insistence on wearing a Speedo to the company's summer pool party.

MATING HABITS: Failing to possess even one smidgen of self-consciousness and propriety, Turkeys are shameless in their pursuit of an intended mate, often resorting to bad pick-up lines: "Knock knock." "Who's there?" "A man stepping into heaven, because you are one hot angel!" (When you respond: "A man stepping into heaven, because you are one hot angel who?" he will have no answer.) A Turkey will endure numerous rejections and sometimes even outright hostility and mocking until the beloved is simply worn down and relents to "just one date."

HABITAT: While Turkeys aren't associated with any particular habitat, you'll never be at a loss to identify one in a crowd, whether he's performing bad stand-up at an open mic night, hovering hammishly in back of a local news reporter's on-location shot, or asking for white zinfandel at a cocktail party.

NEST: Taking his cue from the pages of *MAD* magazine, the Turkey fills his nest with tacky and irritating items: a Pelvis Elvis clock, multiple cans of spray cheese, a cushioned toilet seat, the Clapper, a painting of dogs playing poker, and a Chia Pet.

HOW TO LURE: While there's no surefire way to attract a Turkey, if you're a person who worries about propriety and cringes at social faux pas, be assured this type will be on you like syrup on pancakes.

FLIGHT PATTERN: Just as the tryptophan in a hearty turkey dinner can put you to sleep, dating a Turkey can exhaust even the most patient and intrepid boywatcher. Maybe you've watched him chew with his mouth open one too many times. Or maybe you're tired of the way he hoards mini-shampoos and soaps from hotels. Whatever the final straw, there will come a moment when you know this goose—no, we mean turkey—is cooked.

PRIZED FOR: His persistence. A Turkey is rarely discouraged, whether it's due to an otherworldly ability to withstand disdain or simply an innate obliviousness to the social norms of the rest of humankind.

The Subspecies

The Snapper and Popper
(*Ricekrispius hyperbius*)

Forever high on life, The Snapper and Popper is best identified by his excessive and obnoxious gestures. He's often spotted snapping his fingers and making popping noises as he goes. He can't stop himself from compulsively using "finger quotes" when he talks (even if they're not "relevant"), and he greets people by shooting them the two-fingered point and making a clicking noise with his tongue. The Snapper and Popper buys birthday cards for his friends that say "Hey, Guy!" on the front.

BOY TIP: When breaking up with you, he'll end the conversation with a sweeping "It's over" hand gesture. If you ask why and start crying, he'll shrug his shoulders in an exaggerated fashion and make the "She's cuckoo" finger spiral next to his right temple when you're not looking.

CHARACTERISTIC SONG: "Mack the Knife" by Louis Armstrong.

The Frat Boy Springs Eternal
(Fratticus redux)

The Frat Boy Springs Eternal isn't simply nostalgic about his college days; rather, he persists in acting as if they never ended. He loves to go drinking with the guys and then to hook up with a total stranger, bringing her back to a nest decorated with inflatable beer promotional items and furniture that looks like it belongs in his parents' rumpus room circa 1979. While he may have a bit of a beer belly, he's still agile enough to do a keg stand and talented enough to let out an appreciative belch afterwards.

BOY TIP: Look for him at college basketball games; he's the alumnus with the shaved head, face, and chest painted in school colors.

CHARACTERISTIC SONG: "Tubthumper" by Chumbawamba; "Forever Young" by Rod Stewart.

Nyuk-Nyuk Guy
(*Comedia cornballus*)

Research Tools

Animal House

*

Episodes of
The Three Stooges

*

Steve Martin's antics in
The Jerk

Compared to Nyuk-Nyuk Guy's shtick, the humor on a Bazooka Joe comic seems erudite and witty. With a penchant for canned jokes and catch phrases ("No soup for you!" and the Austin-Powersesque "Yeah, baby!!"), Nyuk-Nyuk Guy ends failed attempts at humor by saying either "Get it?" or yelling "ba-dump-bump-ching!" Groans and a *wah, wah, wah* noise are sure to follow.

BOY TIP: You'll reject him when you get fed up with him saying, "But seriously, folks" at inappropriate times, like when you've just told him you think you're falling in love with him.

CHARACTERISTIC SONG: "The Joker" by Steve Miller; anything by Weird Al Yankovic.

> ### Hatchling Behavior
> The young turkey was the life of kindergarten parties, running around with his pants pulled down.

Turkeys
and the Women Who Love Them . . .

True, a Turkey may not be the most sophisticated man on the planet, and his sense of social decorum is sadly lacking. But if you're the type of girl who's sick of toiling for "The Man" forty hours a week and watching the latest world crisis unfold, you might just gobble up a Turkey's nontraditional antics. Despite the fact that others will be laughing *at* him, not *with* him, you admire his ability to live and let live, perhaps seeking to adopt a bit of that carefree nonchalance in your own life. But as your local bartender can warn you, Wild Turkey's not for everyone. Try him in measured doses, and if your tolerance allows, come November you'll have a Turkey on your plate—and as a date.

Docile woodland companion he's nursed back to health

Clothing made from all-natural fibers and in sweatshop-free conditions

Vegans Unite

Yoga mat to maintain his "flexiboy" physique

Hemp bag from Blueberry Organic Farm Food Co-op

3

Doves

Now will I show myself to have more of the serpent than
the dove; that is, more knave than fool.
—Christopher Marlowe, *The Jew of Malta*

Think releasing a multitude of white doves as a
goodwill gesture at weddings or Olympic cel-
ebrations is a beautiful sentiment? Dove boys
beg (politely) to differ. Indeed, these benevolent
souls would object to the potential animal abuse
ramifications of cramming birds into a box only to
release them outside of their natural habitat. Selfless,
kindhearted, trustworthy, and always forgiving, Dove
boys are the guilty conscience of the male world,
who'd as soon throw themselves in front of a train before they would break your heart. Trust us: After
spending five minutes watching the nightly news
with one of these sweet and sensitive boys, you'll
quickly learn what it sounds like when Doves cry.

PLUMAGE: With his complacent smile and empathetic
eyes, you'll never find a Dove wearing ostentatious,

overpriced labels or politically incorrect clothing, like gym shoes created in third-world sweatshops. Instead, he'll advertise his altruistic tendencies in t-shirt form, with slogans like "Honk for Peace" or "Just Say No to the WTO."

BEHAVIOR: Obeying the Golden Rule to the letter of the law, Doves are excruciatingly kind and nonconfrontational. They spurn tawdry reality television and contact sports, and apologize profusely for pointless nonoffenses like sneezing. When someone offends or violates a Dove (a mugger for instance) he will immediately forgive and forget ("How can I hold a grudge? He must have a family to feed at home."). In extreme cases, Doves have been known to slam on the brakes to avoid hitting a turtle in the road, oftentimes at the expense of being rear-ended.

MATING HABITS: A Dove woos with simple gestures, such as bringing you a bouquet of origami flowers. (He couldn't bear to pick any live ones.) His ideal date? Working an evening at the neighborhood soup kitchen, or laying tile in a Habitat for Humanity project. A Dove can be maddening to argue with as he forever takes the high road, making you look like a crazed, childish lunatic in comparison. ("While I agree I may have hurt your feelings, I wish you would have engaged in an open dialogue about it, rather than shooting off a hurtful e-mail about how you'd like to see me get run over by a semi-truck.")

HABITAT: Doves can be found teaching Sunday School classes, hanging out with abandoned senior citizens at rest homes, saving animals from the brink of euthanasia, running in breast cancer marathons, and organizing charity fund drives for handicapped children.

NEST: Just as a feathered dove's nest is flimsy, with a few sticks seemingly tossed together, a Dove boy's home is idealistically impractical. His fridge is filled only with dolphin-safe tuna and organically grown vegetables, as they're the sole foods that meet his ethical standards, and the living room features a smattering of tacky gifts that don't suit his décor but that he felt too guilty not to display (a pink crocheted Kleenex box cover or a "Hang in There!" kitten poster).

HOW TO LURE: Let him be the saint he tries so hard to be. Fall in front of him and fake an injury. Run up to him crying, telling him you lost your dog. Engage him in a passionate discussion on how you've become disillusioned with the wealthy lifestyles you see in your job. He won't be able to resist coming to your aid.

FLIGHT PATTERN: He can no longer tolerate your "cruel" jokes about Donald Trump's hair; you can no longer handle his heartbreaking sighs at the shabby treatment of Charlie Brown during the Christmas special. ("No one respects his essential humanity—

The Bird, The Boy

Male doves take an active role in parenting their young, sitting on the nest and keeping it warm during the day so that the females can take over at night. Likewise, Dove boys are comfortable being "Mr. Mom," enjoying the opportunity to experience firsthand the "natural and amazing joys of fatherhood," including burping and changing diapers.

they reject him because he's a bald visionary, a modern-day prophet.").

PRIZED FOR: When he says you're beautiful, he means it (because lies, even white ones, are wrong). What's more, when he adopts a starving African child at Sally Struthers's urging, you'll feel virtuous by association. In the end, your wrongs will somehow seem balanced out by his rights.

The Subspecies

Father Theresa
(Patronius saintofpeace)

In college, Father Theresa majored in International Studies and attended feminist rallies and hunger strikes in lieu of keg parties. After a night of lovemaking, you'll find him staring at the ceiling, plagued with guilt over his blissful postcoital state when Tibetan monks and whales have it so bad. If you take him out to dinner, be prepared for sad shakes of the head and frequent sighs as he watches waiters take away half-eaten meals. ("That shrimp cocktail could have fed a family of four in the Sudan.") A frequent volunteer at animal shelters, he's adopted enough three-legged dogs and one-eyed cats to make his home a veritable deformed pet menagerie.

BOY TIP: If you're dating Father Theresa, get comfortable with the idea of a cubic zirconium engagement ring. ("The diamond trade is exploitative and imperialistic!")

CHARACTERISTIC SONG: "Give Peace a Chance" by John Lennon; "Blowin' in the Wind" by Bob Dylan.

The Choir Boy Grown-Up
(Ned flandersium)

A lifelong practitioner of religious faith, the Choir Boy Grown-Up is opposed to sleeping through weekend religious services. He winces every time you say a curse word, and may have a menorah, crucifix, or "Footprints" plaque in his bedroom, making it hard for you to have sex there (God is literally watching). That being said, he's likely to honor the sanctity of your relationship, and won't stray far from home, like some cheatin' ol' prodigal boyfriend.

BOY TIP: Though it may seem difficult to seduce this seemingly chaste guy, appeal to his religious fervor by trying these lines: "I'm thinking of a certain 'hymn' and it's not a song" or "How 'bout coming back to my place for a little bread and wine?"

CHARACTERISTIC SONG: "Like a Prayer" by Madonna; "Send Me an Angel" by the Scorpions.

The Guy Girls Love (But Won't Date)
(Justus friendius)

Just as Duckie from *Pretty in Pink* never stood a chance with Molly Ringwald, this perpetually nice guy gets turned down time and time again for less worthy, less kind, and less dependable men. When he tries to put a move on any number of girl "friends," they all just smile condescendingly, rub his back, and say, "Oh, I wish I knew someone I could fix you up with—you are such a *catch*!" Those same girls' boyfriends are not in the slightest threatened by him, as they regard him as a harmless mascot.

BOY TIP: If you really want to date this one, don't call him "sweetheart" or a similarly benign but nonsexual term. Instead, you've got to recognize the sexy stallion in him where everyone else sees a kiddie carnival horse.

CHARACTERISTIC SONG: "That's What Friends Are for" by Dionne Warwick; "He Ain't Heavy, He's My Brother" by The Hollies.

※

Doves
and the Women Who Love Them . . .

Maybe you're feeling nostalgic for your days in Girl Scouts spent sitting around the campfire singing

"Kumbaya" and weaving friendship bracelets. Or maybe you're a hippie born in the wrong generation, wondering what's so funny 'bout peace, love, and understanding as you hanker for a man who shares your kind-yet-impractical values. Whatever motives prompt this lovey-dovey allure, you'd best take note: While they are as gentle as Johnson's Baby Wash, a Dove's passivity can be incredibly frustrating when it comes to confronting evil bill collectors, nasty in-laws, or rude neighbors. This harsh world requires plenty of gumption, and since your boy's busy placidly roosting on an olive branch, you're gonna have to be the bitch.

✳

As Seen In Nature

Gandhi

*

John Lennon

*

Matthew Cuthbert from *Anne of Green Gables*

*

Friar Laurence from *Romeo and Juliet*

*

Spock

*

Charlie from *Lost*

*

Sam Gamgee from *The Lord of the Rings*

*

Moby

*

Nelson Mandela

*

Bob Ross
("Paint happy trees!")

Byronic flowing locks

Scarf to "preserve his vocal chords" for readings

Dandelions plucked from Walt Whitman's grave

Worn tweed blazer for that "Sexy Prof" appeal

4

Swans

The swan murmurs sweet strains with a flattering tongue,
itself the singer of its own dirge.
— Marcus Valerius Martialis, *Epigrams*

The swan, like the soul of the poet,
By the dull world is ill understood
— Heinrich Heine, *Early Poems—Evening Songs*

Why is a swan's neck so long? Perhaps it's because this glorified goose's head is forever in the clouds. At least that's the case with the boy variety of Swans who are floating through the timeless ether of a world that doesn't quite exist. Seeking the classical perfection once admired by the Romantics and Pre-Raphaelites, Swans have a graceful, sublime quality that's easy to fall for. Like their avian counterparts (who inspired a classical ballet), Swan boys have a way of holding you spellbound as they epitomize a heroic, unsullied aesthetic dreamscape full of metaphorical *pirouettes* and *grande jetés*.

PLUMAGE: With soft ivory skin and a lithe body, the Swan glides more than walks, with eyes that emanate a soulful, faraway gaze, as if he were pondering a Grecian urn amidst the soundtrack of a Strauss waltz. Black turtlenecks, tweed blazers with elbow patches, and weathered brown cords represent the general ilk of his wardrobe.

BEHAVIOR: Emulating the classic ideals of the Romantics, the Swan lives in a vacuum where neither pop culture nor the tacky uncouthness of the masses can reach him. (He thinks *Survivor* is a long-lost tome by Robert Louis Stevenson.) Interested purely in the pursuit of beauty, a Swan can't be bothered by the mundane, pedestrian, or practical. He shuns most technology and fails to keep up with current events (and current fashions). He laments that monocles and spats are not still in vogue. When this prompts you to make a Mr. Peanut joke, he will stare at you blankly. The Swan can be deemed a snob or out of touch by many, but others will admire his grace, finesse, and ability to incorporate words like "alas" and "ergo" into everyday conversation. He speaks a second language fluidly, probably French, German, or Italian.

MATING HABITS: Picturesque displays of romance are part of the Swan's courtship ritual. While ambling down a busy sidewalk, he may suddenly grab you by the shoulders to face him, cradle your face in his hands, and bestow upon you a lengthy tender kiss after uttering a profundity like, "Your stunning visage negates all the world's harshness and sorrow." Or he'll stop you in the middle of the cereal aisle at the supermarket and slow dance with you during a particularly moving rendition of George Michael's "Careless Whisper." After spending the night at his house, you may wake up to realize he's using your naked back as a writing desk as he feverishly completes a sonnet about you.

HABITAT: Nature is the Swan's secondary mistress, so look for him at city parks, reclining near the bank of a lily pond as he chews on the end of a dandelion and ponders the world's truth and beauty. You'll also likely find him at smoky jazz clubs, idly wandering the moss-covered gravestones at historic cemeteries, and touring Europe's great cities on one-man sojourns. He's not at all comfortable in places like fast-food chains or 7-11s, uttering the cry "Death first!" when offered a package of pork rinds.

NEST: Cluttered with the perfectly unkempt detritus of a tortured artist who's trying too hard: a vase of decayed flowers, a candle that has melted itself onto the table, and a half empty bottle of cheap Chianti. His place is old, with high ceilings, hardwood floors, heavy drapes, and a music stand near a drafty window to complete the Bohemian look.

HOW TO LURE: Be poised, graceful, and Audrey Hepburn-ish—the ultimate wood sprite-in-waiting. Wear your hair slicked back in a bun like a dewy-lipped prima ballerina. Be coy and somewhat standoffish, but throw in a degree of neediness for good measure.

(When you see a cockroach or something similarly unseemly, pretend to faint in his arms like the fragile heroine of some Gothic novel.)

FLIGHT PATTERN: Just as legend says that a dying swan exhibits massive histrionics before entering into that good night, the boy version is equally dramatic when it comes to your swan song. He may dump you by leaving a single, long-stemmed red rose at your door with the accompanying haiku scrawled on a dirty Starbucks napkin:

> *Your eyes glimmer with*
> *sorrow. I am sleeping with*
> *your best friend. I weep.*

PRIZED FOR: Making you feel like Dante's Beatrice or Beethoven's "Immortal Beloved." As his muse, you'll believe you *really do* have "gossamer hair and eyes of the finest lapis lazuli."

The Subspecies

Dirty Poet Boy
(Byronicus ironicus)

This wounded wordsmith spends his time writing and reciting poetry that is either completely obscure (referencing Dadaism) or riddled with clichés ("Your love glistens like the dewdrops on a calla lily."). Any and every occasion in his life prompts him to wax poetic; being stuck in a packed subway car without

The feathered variety of this breed mates for life, but a Swan boy's attentions are not nearly so steadfast. Monogamy, to him, is so very bourgeois.

air-conditioning will have him quoting from his masterpiece, "The Crush of Humanity." When you accidentally step in dog crap, he'll race home to compose a sonnet called "As Nature Expires."

BOY TIP: Hunt down a Dirty Poet Boy at some hip underground coffeehouse, then surreptitiously speak to him in iambic pentameter. It'll blow his mind.

CHARACTERISTIC SONG: "Poetry Man" by Phoebe Snow; "Scarborough Fair" by Simon and Garfunkel.

Classical Musician Guy
(Phil harmonicus)

The pensive silent type, Classical Musician Guy speaks mainly through his music. Using a broken pencil stashed behind his ear, he will scribble bits of melody on scraps of paper, then later brood stormily over his piano or cello, pounding out the notes along with life's tensions. You'll either get turned on when he performs a private concert for you or you'll squirm awkwardly with a half-wit grin on your face, praying for him to get it over with already.

BOY TIP: Try to act interested when he's experimenting on a new instrument like the glockenspiel or didgeridoo. It's a phase that will hopefully pass.

CHARACTERISTIC SONG: "Bittersweet Symphony" by The Verve.

No TV Guy
(Mustnotsee teeveeum)

Refusing, for elitist purposes, to own a television set, No TV Guy is frustratingly out of touch with pop culture fabulousness. In group conversations,

As Seen In Nature

Schroeder from the Peanuts' gang

*

Ethan Hawke

*

Daniel Day-Lewis

he's constantly asking for clarification when you're discussing Tony Soprano's therapy sessions or rehashing plot points from last week's *Lost*. Time spent at his house will be tortuously slow as you wile away the hours with more "constructive" wastes of time like playing Scrabble or listening to NPR.

BOY TIP: There's no sense trying to convince him that *The OC* is actually a compellingly campy program worth watching. Rather than stress out about all the shows you're missing when you're hanging out with

Grub

Figs, Stilton cheese, and absinthe.

him, invest in TiVo and worship it like the false God it is.

CHARACTERISTIC SONG: Not "I Want My MTV" by Dire Straits.

✵

Swans
and the Women Who Love Them . . .

If you're in love with a Swan, you're the type of girl who can roam museums for hours, who treats herself to high tea, and who dreams of naming her future children Bronwyn or Waverly. In high school English, while studying the Romantics, you thought you had damn near died and gone to heaven. Ever since, you've tried to "gather ye rosebuds while ye may," which is one of the reasons you're drawn to the lyricism, romance, and intellectual vigor of an impassioned Swan. Enjoy the dreaminess of it all, but just remember that a Swan doesn't want his pristine existence tainted with the Cheetos-like aftertaste and cheesy fingers of the commercialized world. Unless you are truly prepared to forever relinquish your love of *Real World* marathons, Taco Bell, and Adam Sandler movies, the twain (you and the Swan, that is) shall never be one.

✵

5

Songbirds

A light broke in upon my brain—
It was the carol of a bird;
It ceased, and then it came again,
The sweetest song ear ever heard.
—Lord Byron, *The Prisoner of Chillon*

Nightingales sing badly.
—Jean Cocteau, attr.

Whether it's a sibilant *cha-cha-cha,* angry *kip-kip-kipper-kipper,* or nasal *neh-neh-neh,* the varied notes of the North American songbird provide as wide a spectrum of noise as an *American Idol* audition. The Songbird boy is equally varied in musical preference—be it acid jazz, bluegrass, flamenco, or death metal. Yet bird and boy share one driving purpose in life: the obsessive desire to force their music upon every innocent set of ears in the vicinity. Whether he's blaring an obnoxious bass-driven car stereo, enthusiastically strumming guitar for reluctant friends, or singing along with his aggravating new Broadway hits CD, these Tommy Tunes know how to play the songs that make the young girls cry.

PLUMAGE: Like a critically ill patient connected to an oxygen tank, your garden variety Songbird is perpetually tethered to a Walkman or MP3 player. Most prefer to adopt an indie-rock look, sporting band t-shirts over long-sleeved thermal tees and trendy shag cuts, although certain types deviate, opting for a total metalhead 'do.

BEHAVIOR: The consummate performer, a Songbird hates being a mere audience member and prefers to pretend he's *in* the show, playing air guitar along with Jack at a White Stripes concert or murmuring all the lyrics during a particularly moving portion of *Rent*. Even in everyday life, the Songbird is hip to the beat, drumming his fingers excessively on the steering wheel, tapping his silverware upon the table during dinner, or humming along with Muzak in an elevator.

MATING HABITS: The Songbird is drawn to mates who respect musical talent—especially his. He'll make mixes to win over the object of his affection, simultaneously demonstrating an eclectic repertoire ranging from Bach to the Beatles to the Beta Band. He might even serenade you with songs he's written, during which you will either revel in his love or pray the Fat Lady starts singing soon.

HABITAT: Whether it's a record store, concert hall, underground club, or the von Trapp family mountain estate, Songbirds gravitate to any locale that has good acoustics. While a Songbird may proclaim to have backstage access to his favorite band, in most cases, this translates to hours spent waiting at a utility door in an adjacent alley, surrounded by other enthusiastic yet semifrightening groupies.

NEST: With an extensive music library, surround-sound speaker systems, rare concert posters, framed album covers, and a guitar and amp resting in the corner, the Songbird nest is a literal music "mix." He always has music playing, even if he's not at home, and his answering machine is chock full of disgruntled messages from neighbors who have had their fill of his 2 a.m. Jimmy Page impersonations.

HOW TO LURE: Say goodbye to your Dido and Sarah McLachlan CDs, and start worshipping your songster's music of choice, especially if it's his own band. He'll be delighted when you "coincidentally" have his favorite album cued on your car stereo. ("Oh my god, I love this, too! The later stuff is good, but this early stuff, shit, it's raw, it's *it*, you know?") For added help, study the habits of Gwyneth Paltrow or Priscilla Presley, both of whom snagged their own Songbird.

FLIGHT PATTERN: Either his bandmates will start likening you to Yoko Ono, or you'll decide you must maintain your integrity in asserting Van Halen was better *with* David Lee Roth. Either way, he'll dump you on the spot.

PRIZED FOR: When dating a Songbird, you'll actually live *Behind the Music* rather than watching it on VH1. Not everyone gets to go to parties where the drummer from Bad Religion shows up.

The Subspecies

The Local Rock Star
(Tri-statum minihendrix)

Forever planning to move to L.A. or New York to secure an "inevitable" record deal, the Local Rock Star bides his time by stapling homemade flyers to neighborhood telephone poles, toting equipment around town in a beat-up van, and practicing in his parents' garage or basement. While he acts like the next best thing to Keith Richards, talking about his "habit" and the hordes of groupies who want to sleep with him, his usual commission for a local gig amounts to nothing more than free beer from the bar.

BOY TIP: Even though he claims he can smoke a cigarette, strum the guitar, and listen to you talk on the phone at the same time, don't believe him—he's just honed the rhythmic talent of murmuring "uh-huh" at the right conversational beats.

CHARACTERISTIC SONG: "Jukebox Hero" by Foreigner.

I Heart Vinyl Guy
(High fidelityus)

I Heart Vinyl Guy harbors an undying loyalty to the record album, a yen for ratty t-shirts celebrating obscure bands, and a religious-like reverence for the Velvet Underground. He can wax poetic about the merits of Jack Black and Tenacious D, but seethes with rage when launching into tirades about Clear Channel stations ("Tools of Satan") and MTV ("Sucks ass"). Not in a band himself, I Heart Vinyl Guy has been known to practice the drums in private, too humble to try to match the skills of the masters in public.

Chicks They Dig

The Penny Lane Groupie

*

Streisand-in-Training

BOY TIP: When he asks you what your favorite band is, be ready with a secret list conveniently prepared and approved by your local independent record store clerk.

CHARACTERISTIC SONG: "Video Killed the Radio Star" by The Buggles.

The Technopod
(Twoturntables andamicrophonyium)

The Technopod spends many of his waking hours downloading electronically fused versions of soft-rock standards, e.g., "Total Eclipse of the Heart" spliced into a twenty-minute dance mix. Making the notion of live bands obsolete, he uses soundboards to create ambient noise in the vein of the Chemical Brothers. A staple at all-night dance parties, the Technopod whirls himself into a trancelike frenzy, moving to the ever-pounding beat of the synthesizer, only to crawl into bed at 7 a.m. with his head still spinning.

BOY TIP: If you're prone to seizures, the strobe lights and head-throbbing music at his clubs of choice may pose a health risk.

CHARACTERISTIC SONG: "Atomic" by Blondie; "Groove Is in the Heart" by DeeLite.

Mr. Jazz Hands
(One singularsensationless)

Mr. Jazz Hands exudes sparkle and shine rather than the serious, muted tones of the ersatz rock-and-roller. He was a fixture in high school musicals, and despite his seemingly neutered appearance, had no problem finding dates, usually taking his Eliza Doolittle co-star to prom. He believes the art of singing involves "o-ver-ee-NUNC-ee-ate-ing" and can supplement his routines with soft-shoe tap.

BOY TIP: It may seem like obvious advice, but don't necessarily presume heterosexuality for this breed.

CHARACTERISTIC SONG: "Swanee" by George M. Cohan.

✳

Songbirds
and the Women Who Love Them . . .

Whether he's afflicted with disco fever or has a bad case of the Memphis blues, the Songbird can't ever seem to find the pause button for his life soundtrack. He's constantly humming and getting songs stuck in your head, and maybe having "Any Way You Want It" play 24/7 in your brain is too high a price to pay. But may we suggest you reconsider? There's something to be said for dating the guy who every other chick in the audience is screaming over. Heck, you may even get a song named after you, à la Europe's "Carrie" or Starship's "Sara." Perhaps you crave the potential fame, or maybe you just dig how those leather pants give him a seriously Jim Morrison vibe. Whatever your motive, as long as you support his passion, your relationship with a Songbird will never just be a "one-hit wonder."

✳

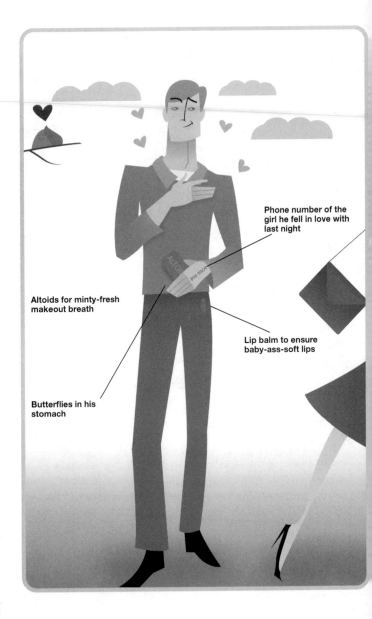

Phone number of the girl he fell in love with last night

Altoids for minty-fresh makeout breath

Lip balm to ensure baby-ass-soft lips

Butterflies in his stomach

6

Lovebirds

O lyric Love, half angel and half bird
And all a wonder and a wild desire.
    —Robert Browning, *The Ring and the Book*

The Lovebird is one hundred percent faithful to his
mate, who is locked in the same cage.
    —Will Cuppy

The epitome of romantic fidelity and affection,
the lovebird is content to nestle affectionately
next to his mate and coo sweet nothings in her
ear. Yet snuggle too close to another living, breathing creature and you might get smothered. Such
is the case with Lovebird boys, those dumbstruck,
starry-eyed romantics. Granted, having forty-three
red roses delivered to your office can be flattering
(one for every day he's known you!). And heartfelt
proclamations, if worded in a non-Air-Supply-lyric
fashion, can be quite moving. However, be warned:
Lovebirds will either make you lovesick with longing and happiness or, depending on your tolerance

for multipage love poems and teddy bear flower bouquets, just plain sick.

PLUMAGE: From knights on white horses to Pepé Le Pew, Lovebirds come in all shapes and sizes. Whatever their daily attire, all share a vapid, swooning look, as if Cupid just hit a bull's-eye straight on their bum. Most are part of a pair, physically connected to a mate via hand and/or tongue.

BEHAVIOR: Eminently qualified to write for schmaltzy greeting card companies, Lovebirds are naturally skilled in the art of pandering elaborate and empty romantic rhetoric. In love with the idea of love, not necessarily any particular girl, Lovebirds are rarely single, as time without a "lovah" just doesn't suit them. For this type, it's all or nothing when it comes to a mate—spending an evening with the guys isn't even a consideration. (He ain't no part-time lover.)

MATING HABITS: Like gum on the bottom of a shoe, Lovebirds fall hard and stick fast, whether the attraction is reciprocal or not. Most drop the "L" bomb on the fourth date, and by the sixth are suggesting names for your unborn children. ("Cody? Madeline?") Don't be surprised to find a few ex-fiancées in the closet, as his unbridled enthusiasm and lack of discrimination in seeking out mates may have backfired in the past.

HABITAT: Look for a Lovebird lip-locked to a girl in a movie theater, leg-entwined with a lover on a blanket at the park, or, in a moment straight from *Lady and the Tramp,* at an Italian restaurant spoon-feeding his lady spaghetti as he slurps from the other side.

NEST: Meet the only male who not only buys decorative frames, but uses them, thoughtfully featuring pictures of the two of you on your cruise to Acapulco and celebrating New Year's 2002 together. With no dearth of soft pillows and silk sheets, his nest is a veritable love shack. If he's currently in a relationship, he'll let his sweetie add her feminine touch with jumbo-sized stinky candles and bowls of pot-pourri.

HOW TO LURE: Be the daughter of his father's arch-nemesis, or live on the wrong side of the tracks. The challenge and allure of being a star-crossed lover will draw him like a moth to the flame.

FLIGHT PATTERN: Like their aviary counterparts, Love-bird boys prefer to mate for life and ignore everyone else in the world, especially the passersby they gross out with inconsiderate public makeout sessions. However, if his partner dies an early tragic death or just gets tired of the responsibility that comes with being someone's "reason for living," he'll mourn the end for a period of time, then promptly move on to the next suitable mate.

PRIZED FOR: Making you feel utterly, totally, completely, and thoroughly loved. Besides, *somebody* has

> ### The Bird, The Boy
>
> Having a lovebird as a pet can be a rewarding experience—that is, if you don't put one in a cage with a smaller bird. Due to their excessive chewing habits, they can harm and even kill other birds. Similarly, a particularly smitten Lovebird can compulsively stroke your hair and nibble your ear to the point of distraction.

to keep fueling the Prince Charming-happily-ever-after myth.

The Subspecies

The Shameless Flirt
(Willoughby wickhamrakeius)

Renowned for making any woman believe she's the meaning in his life *and* the inspiration. Even the most embittered and wary among us aren't immune to his rakish charm and adorable smirk, and within ten minutes of meeting him, are sighing like some love-struck Jane Austen heroine. Despite his initially fevered interest, the second you respond in a genuine way, expect a silence akin to a nuclear winter. For him, it's all about the chase.

BOY TIP: No, that's not a compulsive eyelid tic. It's only the Shameless Flirt's incessant winking, after which he'll seductively mouth "Hi," as if he just stepped out of a cheesy '70s porn flick.

CHARACTERISTIC SONG: "I Want You to Want Me" by Cheap Trick; "Lead Me On" by Teena Marie.

The Determinator
(Failureisnot anoptionus)

Like an unhinged self-help guru, The Determinator believes in the power of positive thinking when it comes to a relationship, whether it's reciprocal or not. If you grudgingly agree to meet him for just one beer at the local pub, he'll bring you a corsage to wear. Subtle blow-off techniques, like non-returned phone calls or the fact that you've blocked his e-mails, are viewed simply as your way of being coy.

BOY TIP: Be firm when rejecting the Determinator. If you give him even the slightest bit of hope (hell freezing over or pigs flying), he'll be knocking at your door for years to come.

CHARACTERISTIC SONG: "I'm Gonna Make You Love Me" by the Supremes; "Never Gonna Give You Up" by Rick Astley.

The Prince of PDA
(Lackius commondecency)

The Prince of PDA and his beloved treat every moment as if it's their last: clutching hands across the brunch table while eating, excessively hugging each other at the airport terminal (even though they're on the same flight), and trying to outdo each other with extravagant declarations of love. ("I love you to infinity." "No, I love you to infinity plus one!") Look for him and his girl making out at the grocery store, whispering sweet nothings during a literary reading, and engaging in private giggling during a funeral.

As Seen In Nature

Seth Cohen on *The OC*

*

Shakespeare's Romeo

*

Sir Lancelot

*

The Tin Man from *The Wizard of Oz*

*

Rick Blaine from *Casablanca*

BOY TIP: It must be pointed out that wherever there's a Prince of PDA, there's a Princess. It takes two to tango.

CHARACTERISTIC SONG: "Love in an Elevator" by Aerosmith; "Never Tear Us Apart" by INXS.

※

Lovebirds
and the Women Who Love Them . . .

If you're looking for a Lovebird, it's likely you suffer a bit from a happily-ever-after complex. Still, you believe that true love really does exist beyond the animated world of Disney, and you're not going to settle until you get it, complete with a dozen roses and a box of chocolates. Frankly, who among us hasn't wished to make sweet love with *Titanic*'s Jack Dawson, even if it comes along with a gun-wielding ex-fiancé, sinking ship, and nasty case of hypothermia? Your stubborn desire to be loved from head to toe, to be worshipped for the lovely girl who you are, gives you a self-confidence and determination that will carry you through many a bad date. When the right Lovebird comes along, you'll express your love everywhere and anywhere—gawkers be damned!

※

Weary eyes reflecting countless sleepless nights

Perpetual five o'clock shadow

Well-worn leather jacket (as battered as his lonely soul)

Harmonica for playing plaintive Dylan tunes on cold winter nights

7

Night Owls

In the twilight of an evergreen thicket sits a great horned owl like a hermit in his cell in pious contemplation of his own holiness and the world's wickedness. But this recluse hates not sin, only daylight and mankind.

—Rowland E. Robinson,
In New England Fields and Woods

The gravest bird's an owl.

—Allan Ramsay, *Scottish Proverbs*

At night, sitting around a campfire, you can hear the question amidst the rustling leaves and howling wind: "Who? Who? Who?" It is the solitary cry of the night owl, probing the darkness on his existential and melodramatic quest for meaning and companionship. So, too, the Night Owl boy—crying lonely notes of a personality misunderstood—the maligned geniuses, rugged loners, wild-eyed prophets, and, well, let's be honest . . . grade-A freaks of the boy world. Your mom might not appreciate the fact that the artistry in a Night Owl's tattoos rivals most of the pieces in the Louvre. And your dad probably won't be keen on his role as a founding member of Hackers Against Capitalism. But if you can get beyond a Night Owl's antisocial behavior and penchant for reveling in the witching hours, inside you'll find a wounded soul desperately hoping to be led out of the shadows and into the sunshine of your love.

PLUMAGE: Night Owls prefer the anonymity afforded them by dark plumage, seeking out black denim, used flannel shirts, and work or combat boots. In keeping with his instinctual antipathy for all things daytime-related, the Night Owl sports a perpetual five o'clock shadow. Try as you may, you will be sorely pressed to find even one item in his closet that he could wear to a job interview or cocktail party.

BEHAVIOR: For a Night Owl, one is the loneliest number, as he lives in a state of near 24/7 isolation. Most choose to be alone after years of childhood persecution for being different—e.g. facing extreme ostracism for living on the wrong side of the tracks. As a result, Night Owls judge the rest of mankind as not worth their time, forming hard shells of scorn to protect their vulnerable inner child. Don't expect your friends and family to warm up to a Night Owl: While you see him as simply misunderstood, they'll likely see him as aloof, off-putting, and possibly a serial killer.

MATING HABITS: Hardened by years of loneliness or simply suffering from severe sweaty palms, Night Owls are reluctant to open up to any potential mate. Instead, they seek out those with equally antisocial tendencies, grudgingly accepting such companionship while secretly worshipping their dream girls from afar: the Molly Ringwald *Breakfast Club* prisses or lovely opera stars named Christine. If he does date, don't expect standard candle-lit dinners and roses. Rather, brace yourself for breathtaking, if somewhat frightening, gestures of artistic affection, e.g. painting your name a hundred times upon his bare skin.

HABITAT: Night Owls are solitary creatures, avoiding flocks of people whenever possible. Lone specimens can be found secreted away in artist lofts in abandoned industrial parks or "madman chic" cabins in the deep woods. When they do emerge, they frequent desolate Edward Hopper–esque diners and take long road trips through the desert on a horse with no name.

NEST: An opportunistic nester just like his feathered brother, a Night Owl will make do with whatever's at hand, as long as it provides shelter from the elements. Accommodations include a ratty mattress on the floor, a stark curtainless shower, dirty ashtrays, books by exiled writers, and a space heater—necessitated either by the lack of central heat or unpaid electric bills.

The Bird, The Boy

The outsider of the bird world, an owl is frequently the victim of mobbing; flocks of small birds band together to peck, taunt, and torment the wise old fellow, driving him out of the vicinity. Similarly, as children, most Night Owl boys faced bullying from gangs of classmates, victimized, perhaps, for being just a bit too enthusiastic about a science fair project or for kissing the rich kid's girlfriend after school.

HOW TO LURE: With his endemic shyness, a Night Owl is never a pursuer but forever the pursued. You'll need to gently lure him out of the darkness with simple and familiar gestures, such as inviting him to an Andrei Tarkovsky film festival or offering him a clove cigarette when his own box is empty.

FLIGHT PATTERN: One night, he says he loves you. The next, terrified at the thought of needing someone, he'll miss the date intentionally, exiling himself once again to the familiar territory of "I am a rock, I am an island."

PRIZED FOR: The disapproving stares he'll elicit from the planning committee when you tote him and his Walt Whitman–like beard to your high school reunion. (You never could stand those uptight girls to begin with.)

The Subspecies

Desperado
(Legacy johnwayneium)

Forever hardened by a hurtful past (perhaps the tragic death of a young fiancée), the Desperado seeks solace in the harsh elements, electing to live in rough country, bathe in icy mountain streams, and drive a rusty pickup with only one other companion—a dog named Buck. From 9–5, he can be found working cattle on a dude ranch or manning a lone fire tower in a national forest. After hours he's a fixture at the local dive, drinking hard liquor on the house, courtesy of a weathered bartender named Flo.

BOY TIP: While you may think you're the woman who can make him love again, most of these boys are as tough to crack as big, fat, uncrackable things, and for added bonus, they bring along a world of heartbreak and oftentimes problematic gender assumptions. ("Cuttin' wood's a man's job!")

CHARACTERISTIC SONG: "Lonely Boy" by Paul Anka; "Nature Boy" by Nat King Cole.

The Recluse Artist
(Ear cutter-officus)

The Recluse Artist answers the siren call of his artistic muse at all hours of the night, displaying an otherworldly ability to operate on a mere hour of sleep, which may or may not be facilitated by liberal doses of amphetamines. That's not to say he doesn't have his down times, one minute crying with joy over his newest work, the next, slashing the canvas with a butcher knife and falling to the floor in painful wails. In the true spirit of art as political gesture, the Recluse Artist refuses to sell or display anything he creates. ("Genius can't be commodified by capitalism.")

BOY TIP: Two words for you: Diego Rivera. Passionate artists make lousy boyfriends.

CHARACTERISTIC SONG: "Vincent" by Don Maclean; "Paint It Black" by the Rolling Stones

The Hacker
(*ControlAltDeletium conspiritas*)

Known in the online community by his gaming screen name, Yoda_sorcererstar, the Hacker is a fixture in college computer labs and cyber cafes. He wears heavy metal t-shirts and function-over-form eyeglasses, and attaches multiple pagers and cell phones to his belt as if it were a holster and he were Gary Cooper starring in the techie version of *High Noon*. All through the night, he can be found either downloading *Simpsons* episodes or furiously chatting online, his terminal-lit silhouette a lonely figure amidst the otherwise darkened windows of his parents' house.

BOY TIP: No need to impress a Hacker with the latest looks from *Vogue:* If you dress like Scully or wear a Princess Lea 'do, you'll have him in the palm of your hand.

CHARACTERISTIC SONG: "Hip to Be Square" by Huey Lewis; "I Am the Walrus" by the Beatles.

Solitary Man
(Thecheese standsaloneium)

The Solitary Man doesn't need a band of cohorts to feel comfortable out in public. Not only can he fly solo at bars, restaurants, and movies, he prefers it this way. You can find him pensively studying a chessboard in a smoky, dim coffee shop (a moot point: *who* or even *where* his partner is). Or look for him skulking in the corner of a late-night diner while reading dense theoretical treatises, a neon sign in the background casting intermittent shadows on his well-defined cheekbones.

Research Tools

Phantom of the Opera

*

Edward Scissorhands

*

Donnie Darko

*

Rebel Without a Cause

BOY TIP: He loathes coquettish, girly behavior in women, so don't even think about throwing him your "coy" routine. If your skirt and Jimmy Choos prevent you from hopping on the back of his motorcycle and riding off into the black of night, he'd just as soon leave you in his dust.

Grub

Night Owl boys subsist solely on instant coffee and nicotine, opting to pass on foods with tryptophan.

CHARACTERISTIC SONG: "You Belong to the City" by Glenn Frey; "I Wear My Sunglasses at Night" by Corey Hart.

✳

Night Owls
and the Women Who Love Them . . .

If you think you can make it work with a Night Owl, odds are you've developed a monstrously naïve optimism after watching one too many John Hughes movies during your formative years. To put it simply, a relationship with a Night Owl isn't exactly a bed of roses. Loving one takes the patience of Homer's Penelope, a Winona Ryder–like attraction for antisocial weirdos, and a resolve that rivals even the most determined superhero. That said, if you're the type of girl who's enthralled by the eerie mystique of a quiet, deep thinker ostracized by the rest of the world, then stock up on No-Doz, and prepare for hours and hours of dreamy pillow talk with your Night Owl.

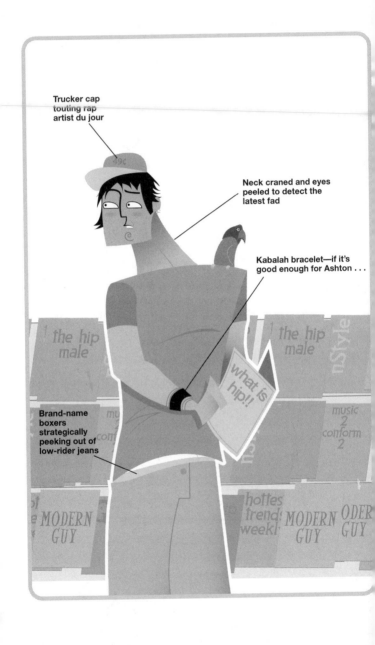

Trucker cap touting rap artist du jour

Neck craned and eyes peeled to detect the latest fad

Kabalah bracelet—if it's good enough for Ashton . . .

Brand-name boxers strategically peeking out of low-rider jeans

8

Parrots

Boys parrot what they hear.
—T. Holcroft, *The Memoirs of Bryan Perdue*

Talk is "cheep." A parrot may be the darling of the bird world for its ability to elocute "Polly wanna cracker" and "Pretty bird, pretty bird," yet one would hardly engage it in any intellectual debates of the *Crossfire* variety. Indeed, this motormouth is only capable of spouting off inane phrases it doesn't understand. The Parrot boy is no less of a living, breathing mimicry machine. Displaying unoriginal thoughts and ideas, he'll hop on any bandwagon that comes his way. True, he walks the walk perfectly, clearly well versed in all the current trends, fashion, and slang terminology. But make no mistake: This rip-off artist wouldn't think of blinking without first checking to see if everyone else is doing it.

PLUMAGE: A slave to the fashion of the day, this label whore's look is trendy and mutable according to what the rest of his posse is wearing, not to mention the "celebrity looks" he's emulating. One day it's a Von Dutch hat, the next it's Original Penguin shirts in every color. In the past, he's mimicked the pocket-chain aesthetic (a la *Swingers*) and the spiky hair look (I'm in a boy band!). Just as a bird has extreme neck mobility beyond 180 degrees, the Parrot boy is forever craning his neck to check out the plumage of those around him. ("Hey man, where'd you get those silver Pumas?")

BEHAVIOR: Forever following the flock, the Parrot takes his cue from others. Consumed with celebrity, he likes to mirror what today's "It" crowd is doing, saying, and wearing. Like an echo in a canyon, listen for him to repeat things his good buddies may have mentioned days or even hours before. He also spews forth intellectual bullshit he picked up from some best-selling book or cable talk show and claims it as his own. ("Well, you know, I've always said that until Pakistan and India can, like, establish a dé-tente, nuclear proliferation will continue to, uh, escalate.")

MATING HABITS: Once all his friends have significant others, he'll follow suit and find a girlfriend, too, looking for the "cookie-cutter beauty" his peers approve of. If you're that girl, he'll start to adopt your tastes (both likes and dislikes) in true "Kling-on" fashion. The imitation may seem flattering and fun at first but soon turns annoying when he echoes everything you say with "Me, too!" and "I *totally* agree." (Such agreement is generally harmless, unless he chimes an "Amen" to your gripes about periods or your childhood obsession with Menudo.)

HABITAT: Likes to travel in packs and will congregate at the local hot spots where there's a red rope and people waiting to get in. He'll definitely be checking out the new movie "everyone's talking about" and is always up to speed on the latest Zagat Guide reviews, since he usually needs someone else's opinion about where he should go.

NEST: The Parrot's dwelling place is a testament to a life spent emulating others. There are plenty of magazines strewn everywhere to keep him au courant. He has the latest everything—mass-market novels and CDs from flash-in-the pan bands. A large-screen TV sits in his home like some sort of altar where he can worship the gods of celebrity and let American advertisers preach him the good news of consumerism.

HOW TO LURE: Be an avant garde trendsetter worthy of emulation. Layer skirts and dresses over jeans, buy stiletto-heeled rubber flip-flops, carry an initialed jelly purse, wear a "right hand" diamond ring, get your German Shepherd a pair of puppy Uggs, and monitor Beyoncé's hairdo daily to ensure your tresses forever reflect hers. Consider even more extreme options like getting a heart-shaped "Jewel Eye" surgically implanted on your eyeball. (It's all the rage in Holland right now.)

The Bird, The Boy

Just as the parrot feeds its young by regurgitating bits of seed and fruit into the mouths of its offspring, the plagiaristic Parrot boy is equally adept at regurgitating points of view and anecdotes which are not of his own creation.

FLIGHT PATTERN: When you no longer fit his profile of "cool girlfriend" he'll kick you to the curb. Be particularly wary of his friends and associates. If even one of them knocks you, you'll soon be last week's flavor.

PRIZED FOR: His monkey-see, monkey-do versatility. He can reinvent himself based on what the rest of his flock is doing and can mix in well with any new group of people, from politicos to potheads, simply by mimicking their behavior.

The Subspecies

The Intellectual Poseur
(Cerebellum imposterum)

Perhaps attempting to mask his own insecurities, the Intellectual Poseur spews out lofty rhetoric that is wholly unoriginal and obviously stolen from a source other than his own mind. He subscribes to *The New Yorker*, which he carries everywhere as a sort of calling card—yet curiously, you've only seen him skim the cartoons. His high-minded political stances are hypocritical as he decries America's dependence on foreign oil while trucking about town in an SUV. Claims to have read *Infinite Jest* by David Foster Wallace and Thomas Pynchon's *V* in their entirety. (Yeah, right.)

BOY TIP: Don't challenge him to source the statistics he rants and raves about, and refrain from pointing out that his little idea for solving the deficit crisis was lifted verbatim from a recent episode of *Frontline*.

CHARACTERISTIC SONG: "Say You, Say Me" by Lionel Ritchie; "I Heard It Through the Grapevine" by Marvin Gaye.

The GQ Rip-Off Artist
(Esquireum aspireum)

Trying desperately to be the "ultimate bachelor," this type considers men's magazines to be his Bible. In his closet are square-toed shoes with buckles and a seersucker suit he bought after *Esquire* deemed it a "staple of every man's wardrobe." From tomes like *Maxim* and *FHM*, he has learned how to "pleasure a woman," and he's currently considering calf implants due to an enlightening article in the June *Men's Health*. He swirls and sniffs wine (even Manischewitz) and likes to order manly cocktails like Dewar's on the rocks.

BOY TIP: While he may appear to be a bit of a dandy, don't rule out what the good book (*GQ*) has taught this rip-off artist. It can be nice to date a guy who takes care of himself—and you'll always have someone to go get a manicure with.

CHARACTERISTIC SONG: "I'm Too Sexy" by Right Said Fred.

El Hiperati
(Blogboy extemporaneous)

Appealing to a sense of irony, El Hiperati follows in the wake of all things "indie." He sports a layered shag haircut and wears clothes acquired from painstaking hours of combing thrift store racks for that perfectly nonchalant hipster look. With a sense of detached amusement, he'll partake in seemingly low-class activities like attending monster truck rallies or drinking Colt 45 in bars hitherto only frequented by Vietnam vets. *The Onion* and *McSweeney's* comprise his daily reading material, and he tends to roost in low-rent-but-soon-to-be-gentrified hipster enclaves.

BOY TIP: Expect cheap but unique gifts presented as part of El Hiperati's courtship ritual, e.g., a used romance novel or a box of Cheerios.

CHARACTERISTIC SONG: "Bohemian By the Numbers" by the Minor Leagues.

Suburban Homeboy
('Sup-yo-yo-ium)

Though he was raised in a very upscale, entitled environment, the Suburban Homeboy has appropriated urban culture into his own "gated community" lifestyle, preferring to act as though he just stepped straight out of Compton. He refers to things as "dope," and may totally weird out an African-American stranger on the street, greeting him with, "Peace, my brothah!" Has souped up his parents' old minivan with subwoofers, spinning rims and hydraulic pumps, but can't seem to scrape off the remains of the "My son's an honor student at River Elementary School" bumper sticker.

BOY TIP: When he calls you his "bitch," it's a term of endearment. Nevertheless, servers at the local Applebee's may be alarmed when he orders the mozzarella sticks "for me and my bitch with extra hizzouse dressing, yo."

Hatchling Behavior

Like the protagonist in an Afterschool Special, the young Parrot was forever prone to peer pressure, willingly stealing a toke from the cool kid's joint or acting upon his gym mates' coaxing to snap the new girl's training bra.

CHARACTERISTIC SONG: "Ice, Ice Baby" by Vanilla Ice; "Informer" by Snow.

❄

Parrots
and the Women Who Love Them . . .

They say imitation is the sincerest form of flattery, and maybe that's why you always tend to fall for Parrots, the guys who not only listen to what you say but can spout it back verbatim. You like someone who can keep pace with today's fast-moving culture and ever-changing trends, even if he's using his own version of Cliffs Notes to do it. What's more, you dig a man with some semblance of mutability—the dude who's just as comfortable in a room full of WASP-y Republicans as he is at a rave. While a Parrot is usually ahead of the curve in terms of what's hot and what's not, you'll have to forgive some of his past lapses in judgment. (He really *did* think the PT Cruiser was going to be the next Porsche, after all.) A Parrot may not have an original bone in his body, but like the Kate Spade bag you got from a street vendor in SoHo, sometimes knockoffs aren't such a bad thing.

❄

As Seen In
Nature

Vanilla Ice

*

Ashton Kutcher

*

Corey Feldman

*

Ryan Seacrest

*

Kevin Federline
(aka Mr. Britney Spears)

*

Sean (P. Diddy/Puffy)
Combs

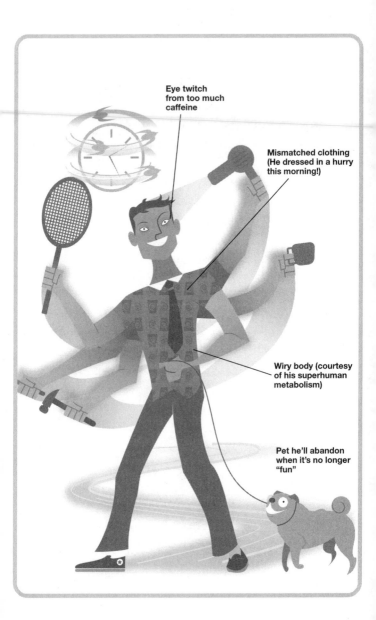

Eye twitch
from too much
caffeine

Mismatched clothing
(He dressed in a hurry
this morning!)

Wiry body (courtesy
of his superhuman
metabolism)

Pet he'll abandon
when it's no longer
"fun"

9

Hummingbirds

See the hummingbird, there, not there.
—Ray Bradbury, *Zen in the Art of Writing*

S unning by the pool on a lazy summer after-
noon, you suddenly hear an irritating buzz
near your ear. Eyes closed, you try swatting it
away, thinking it's just a big bug. But the noise is
neverending. You open your eyes, and there, darting
manically about, is a Hummingbird. Granted, this
particular specimen is a full-grown man who's about
as dainty as a pair of size 16 clodhoppers. Yet with
his frenzied gesticulations and his inability to stay
rooted in one place for more than a nanosecond, he
makes an ADHD-Roadrunner look like Cool Hand
Luke. It's not hard to see why men this hyper and intense share a name with the spazzes of the aviary
world. Fall for one and you'll develop a whole new
appreciation for Ritalin.

PLUMAGE: Like the real hummingbird, which beats its
wings up to eighty times a second, the Hummingbird

boy flits about so quickly that it's difficult to nail down any singular Hummingbird style. Constantly changing his facial hair status from clean shaven to full beard to goatee to Fu Manchu, he mixes up fashion styles just as schizophrenically, one day sporting the disheveled professor look—the next, Sweaty Gym Guy aesthetic. Suffice it to say he dresses in a hurry, wearing whatever's on hand. (Don't expect gym shoes to be tied. Do expect socks to be mismatched.)

BEHAVIOR: Not a subscriber to the "haste makes waste" philosophy, the Hummingbird is perpetually on the move, literally and figuratively. He jumps here and there from one fascination to the next: bee keeping, touring the professional billiards circuit, learning to read Braille. So absorbed is he in what he's doing that he frequently mumbles to himself, à la crazy man on the subway. While he makes up to seventeen phone calls per hour (using speed dial, of course), he doesn't stay on the line long, employing phrases like "Gotta run!" and "Catch ya later" after just thirty seconds. In waiting rooms, board meetings, and lengthy cross-country flights, he impatiently taps his leg and cracks his knuckles one by one, then tries to calm himself by loudly gulping Red Bull, Jolt, or triple espressos.

MATING HABITS: Catch his eye and he'll pursue you with reckless abandon, memorizing the names and ages of your twenty nieces and nephews, reading every book by your favorite author, and relating stories from your past that even you had forgotten ("It's like that time you wet your pants in first grade!"). Once you're a couple, his unbridled zest for life will make you feel lazy and slothlike. Forget snuggling on the couch to watch a nine-hour Orson Welles movie marathon. Instead, you'll be kayaking down Class V rapids, then off to a night of insane club hopping. (Incidentally, you'd think all that energy would give him some extra oomph in the sack, but sadly, this minuteman isn't interested in taking his time. He needs his shut-eye so he can be "up-and-at-em" at the break of day.)

HABITAT: Anywhere and everywhere, though he doesn't perch for too long in one place. You won't find him milling around in restful environments, picnicking in the park, or reading at a coffee shop. Rather, seek him out in places that require intense physical activity (indoor rock-climbing venues), at centers of arcane knowledge (the Mayan antiquities department at the local university), or testing out a gadget (scouring the beach for coins with a new metal detector).

NEST: The Hummingbird nest is filled with discarded items from past obsessions: dead bonsai trees, an empty tropical fish aquarium, and numerous unused infomercial products like the Miracle Thaw or the Ab Roller. He'll never stay in any one nest for too long, moving from city to city, crashing at friends'

The Bird, The Boy

The only bird in the world that can fly sideways and backwards, hummingbirds mirror their human counterparts' ability to jump from interest to interest without losing a beat employing even one transitional phrase or segue. Take your eye off a Hummingbird boy for even a second and he's likely to dart away for good.

houses, and often leaving a devoted pet behind. (Mr. Whiskers was just a passing fancy, after all.)

HOW TO LURE: You're likely to find this species at speed-dating clinics, but if that doesn't pan out, take a tip from the female hummingbird, who remains still during courtship as the male frantically encircles her. Pretend to listen to the buzz of his metaphorical wings, nodding eagerly as he yammers on about how he recently discovered the healing properties of rose quartz or how he's created a new stadium sport—a fusion of golf and jai alai. The longer you can manage to hold his attention, the better your chance of capturing it for good.

FLIGHT PATTERN: As quick to leave as he is to love, the Hummingbird will dump you to find a more enthusiastic mate, ending your relationship as abruptly as it started. ("Unlike you, she gets me. She understands why polka dancing means something to me and to the world.")

PRIZED FOR: His single-minded, albeit temporary, enthusiasm. Hummingbirds make fervent and impassioned recruiters for political campaigns, environmental movements, and cults.

The Subspecies

Manic Hobby Guy
(Hobbyius fickelium)

Whether he's collecting Coca-Cola memorabilia, raising iguanas, practicing Krav Maga, or starting his own dot.com company, Manic Hobby Guy jumps from interest to interest like a cricket on speed. He pours lots of cash into his passion, even if it means outfitting a room in his home as a wood shop, but once the fascination has passed (and it will), the accoutrements are abandoned, simply (saw)dust in the wind.

BOY TIP: Just as he gets bored with his rare orchids and leaves them to shrivel up and die, Manic Hobby Guy will soon tire of you, leaving the sweet flower of your love to wither. Maintain his interest by mixing things up: Try out a British accent or adopt a new pseudonym. ("Forget Jill. Call me Anastazia.")

CHARACTERISTIC SONG: "Can't Stand Still" by AC/DC; "Manic Monday" by The Bangles.

The Job Jumper
(*Curriculumvitae redux*)

Known in college as the Major Changer, the Job Jumper makes frequent and dramatic career shifts, aspiring to hotel management one week, then deciding he must move to a Buddhist ashram the next. Whatever job he's currently in "depresses and oppresses" him, and he'll quit steady work at the drop of a hat to become a sport fisherman in Baja or a Texas rodeo clown (adding yet another entry to his already four-page-long resume). The Job Jumper may possess a bachelor's degree in business, but after a month working a 9–5 finance job, he'll decide it's not his calling and will reenroll for an oh-so-practical philosophy degree.

BOY TIP: Be forewarned: A regular paycheck, hefty 401(k), and health benefits are not the Job Jumper's forte. It takes a special woman with a steady job to support both herself and his dream-hopping.

Hatchling Behavior

Spastically enthusiastic even at a young age, a Hummingbird was adept at mobilizing impressionable neighborhood children to help him run successful ventures, from Choose-Your-Own-Flavor Kool-Aid stands to dramatic productions of plays he authored.

"Changes" by David Bowie; "I Still Haven't Found What I'm Looking For" by U2.

The Health Nut
(Slimgoodbodyum extremus)

The Health Nut is obsessed with the latest fitness trend, popping antioxidant vitamins and wearing a pedometer everywhere he goes. He's tried Atkins ("A crustless pizza, please . . ."), raw diets ("When you cook eggs, you lose most of the protein."), and calorie-restricted diets ("Eating only three rice cakes a day activates my biological survival mechanisms!"). You can find him practicing the newest extreme fitness craze, from Ultimate Rollerblade Frisbee to Tag-Team Underwater Pilates.

As Seen In Nature

Ferris Bueller

*

Tigger

*

Jamie Foxx

*

Burt from *Mary Poppins*

*

Kramer from *Seinfeld*

BOY TIP: At parties, he's a buzzkill, loudly eschewing all alcohol and soft drinks ("They're toxins!"), and leaving early because he's hitting the gym at five the next morning. Dinner dates involve you either partaking in his tree-bark cuisine, or eating a burger and feeling like a disrespectful, body-poisoning fat ass.

CHARACTERISTIC SONG: "Let's Get Physical" by Olivia Newton John; "I Feel Good" by James Brown.

❋

Hummingbirds
and the Women Who Love Them . . .

If you love a Hummingbird, it's safe to say that the extreme dips and curves of life's roller coasters won't ever throw you for a loop. Unfazed as you are by the fluctuating whims of a hyperactive spaz, your personality must either be equally rambunctious or as calming as a nice warm Calgon bath. You're never put off by playing supporting actress, if not stage manager, to your guy's newest project. And while you may not be hankering to base jump from the Golden Gate Bridge, there's something of a thrill-seeker lurking deep inside you. After all, you're attracted to a whirling dervish of a man, one who can make even MacGyver's ever-spinning creative wheels seem stale and hackneyed.

❋

Bizarre Bird Fact

These feathered whippersnappers vary in size, from the Giant Hummingbird of South America, which weighs twenty grams, to the tiny Bee Hummingbird, which is about the size of a bumblebee. Likewise, the wingbeats of different types can vary from ten to eighty beats per second.

Sloping shoulders from carrying the weight of the world.

Complexion remarkably free of laugh lines

Arms crossed in a defensive stance

Solemn trench coat for protection from impending Apocalypse

10

Grouse

Take one look at a male sage grouse performing his mating dance—his spiky tail feathers erected, yellow eye combs flashing and olive green air sacs ballooning from his chest—and you will know why Meriwether Lewis and William Clark dubbed it the "cock of the plains."

—Rene Ebersole, "Saving the Sage Grouse,"
National Wildlife Federation

Like Atlas, who supposedly carried the weight of the world on his shoulders, the Grouse boy feels equally put upon, sighing and harrumphing his way through life as if he's doing the universe some giant favor. Just as the bird he's named for tends to be generally elusive and unapproachable, these malcontents are equally alienating with their sorry attitudes, constant criticism, and generally bleak outlook. Even life's most beautiful things—a newborn baby, a brilliant sunset, a recording of Louis Armstrong's "What a Wonderful World"—all prompt the Grouse's indignantly negative and doleful remarks. In short, he's the world's biggest party pooper.

PLUMAGE: Easily identified by his rolling eyes; grimacing face; sulky, slouchy posture; and crossed arms, the Grouse is forever complaining about his clothing, be it a sweater that itches too much or socks that make his toes feel "claustrophobic." And just as the sage grouse of the American prairie inflates its unique chest air sacs as part of its histrionics, the Grouse boy is equally prone to huffing and puffing.

BEHAVIOR: Whether he's whining, sulking, or bellyaching, the attitude-laden Grouse forever rains on people's parades and spoils the party. Upon seeing that "I'd Like to Teach the World to Sing" Coke commercial, he'll remark, "That's *so* fake. That would *never* happen." He'll similarly debunk the Tooth Fairy in the presence of children and mock couples who throw coins in a wishing well. Not exactly a people person, the most positive phrase you'll ever hear him utter is, "It's all right, I guess." He particularly enjoys ridiculing the things you most love, from movies to authors to musical taste. ("What, are you *kidding me?* Sting sucks!")

MATING HABITS: Dating a Grouse is a true lesson in patience and martyrdom. After complaining endlessly that there's nothing to do, he'll balk at your suggestions and then accuse you of abandoning him when you dare to make plans without him. Any gift from a Grouse will be prefaced by the disclaimer, "I'm sure you won't like it." Convey genuine feelings of tenderness for this breed and he'll snicker sarcastically in response. On dates, his refusal to tip generously may leave you mortified, as does his justification: "What? You don't see anyone tipping *me* for being a bank teller!"

HABITAT: While he occasionally ventures out to dive bars, smoky coffee shops, and depressing film festivals, he prefers to languish and brood from the comforts of home. Besides, he doesn't believe the outside world has much to offer that will impress him. His excursions are accompanied by customary whining: "I hate crowds!" or "I knew traffic would be a nightmare!"

NEST: With drawn shades, an unmade bed, and dirty dishes in the sink, the Grouse doesn't have time to keep his place tidy. He's far too busy writing letters of complaint to local business establishments and reading existentialist texts and conspiracy theory books.

HOW TO LURE: Adopt a comic cynicism he'll find sexy and be sure to bandy about key sarcastic phrases such as, "Yeah, right," "Whatever," and "Gee, *thanks*." Either that, or hunker down and be a regular Pollyanna in the hopes of creating the biggest psychological breakthrough since the Grinch acquired his Yuletide cheer.

FLIGHT PATTERN: Sick of his negative attitude and constant bitching, you'll end things. First, he'll respond with sarcasm: "Boo-hoo. Big loss!" Then, he'll move on to ridiculous pathos: "Why don't you just make me drink Clorox next time? It'd be less painful! Are you happy now?!" He'll be left forever feeling that love is a sham. (No, wait—he thought that already.)

PRIZED FOR: Those times when his cynical remarks are a laugh riot—like when you're watching the latest J. Lo cinematic stink bomb or mocking the clothing of local TV news anchors.

The Subspecies

The Constant Complainer
(Mitch bitchmoanium)

The only boy who can make dining out as painful and mortifying as getting a root canal in the nude, the Constant Complainer won't hesitate to send food back or ask to speak with the manager. He'll demand his money returned when he didn't particularly enjoy a movie, and he'll storm out to berate his neighbors if they so much as cough after 10 p.m. Occasionally threatens lawsuits but has never followed through on them.

BOY TIP: Once you start dating him, be prepared for your social invitations to quickly dwindle. Your friends and acquaintances won't want to deal with his kvetching, and you'll become a pariah by association.

CHARACTERISTIC SONG: "Can't Be Satisfied" by Muddy Waters.

Mr. Mopey
(Eeyore existentialis)

Rainy days, Mondays, and just about every other day gets this type down, and while there

As Seen In Nature

Shakespeare's Hamlet

*

Dennis Miller

*

Charlie Brown (when he's in the dumps)

*

Denis Leary

is no apparent reason for his despondency, he will not hesitate in bringing you into his quagmire of baffling sadness. Heavy sighing and a hangdog face could be the result of pondering man's inhumanity to man or hearing that tonight's *Law & Order* is a repeat. Whatever is troubling Mr. Mopey, don't expect him to do anything to remedy the situation. He may often take the pensive stance of Rodin's *The Thinker* as he ponders why the world is "such a shitty place."

BOY TIP: Often, Mr. Mopey's woe-is-me attitude is just a subtle cry for attention. Sometimes, simply rubbing his head, giving him a huge hug, and offering him control of the TV remote will snap him out of it.

CHARACTERISTIC SONG: "Creep" by Radiohead; "I'm Down" by the Beatles.

The Cynic
(Sarcastius crabassius)

Forever stripping the silver lining from every cloud, the Cynic thinks emotions like hope and joy are for simpletons. At weddings he'll whisper "I give 'em three years, tops" and when you congratulate him on a promotion he'll say: "It won't matter much when they outsource my job to India." The Cynic is most sarcastic at times of increased emotion, like his father's funeral. ("Leave it to Dad to have picked the cheapest coffin!")

BOY TIP: He believes bringing children into this world is a selfish act that contributes to the problem of overpopulation, so if you're hankering for rug rats, this isn't your guy.

CHARACTERISTIC SONG: "Losing My Religion" by REM.

Ripped off Santa's beard the first time he sat on his lap.

❉

Grouse
and the Women Who Love Them . . .

If you love a Grouse, consider getting your therapist's license. After all, you're certainly willing to nod and listen with a calm, gentle demeanor as your guy complains and relates how the world has abused and misused him. Not that he's all bad. Remember, the squeaky wheel gets the grease, so when dating a Grouse, you won't have to settle for the worst table at the restaurant or put up with people behind you talking during a movie. And believe it or not, some Grouse actually have a pretty hilarious sense of humor, sarcastic and negative as it may be. It's quite possible that with a little sweet love and affection from a cheerful chick like yourself, the Grouse may eventually lose some of his gruffness and adopt just a bit of your optimistic outlook on life. Be the Edith Bunker to his Archie, the Dharma to his Greg, the Ernie to his Bert, and somehow, just maybe, you can turn that curmudgeon into a tolerable companion.

❉

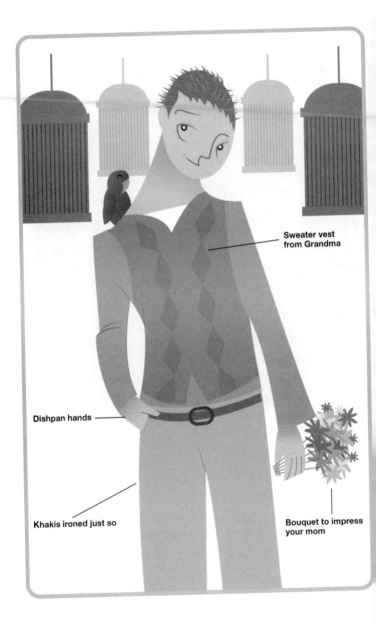

Sweater vest
from Grandma

Dishpan hands

Khakis ironed just so

Bouquet to impress
your mom

11

Parakeets

'Tis almost morning; I would have thee gone;
And yet no further than a wanton's bird,
Who lets it hop a little from her hand,
Like a poor prisoner in his twisted gyves,
And with a silk thread plucks it back again,
So loving-jealous of his liberty.
—Shakespeare, *Romeo and Juliet*

Whether they've never been cut from their mother's apron strings or simply enjoy wearing an apron themselves, Parakeets are sweet-natured homebodies who rarely buck the rules or raise a fuss. Like their caged counterparts in living rooms across America, these domestic and docile men feel no need to test their wings' limits or sow wild oats. Some shack up with a domineering girlfriend who officially rules the roost. Others may continue to nest with good ol' Mom and Dad. Regardless, these ever-obliging creatures crave companionship and the comforts of a clean, warm bed. Whether their compliant, stay-at-home nature is innate or learned, Parakeet boys are the ideal house pet. He may not sit on your finger, but he'll surely be wrapped around it.

PLUMAGE: Generally clean cut, well-pressed, and spit-polished to perfection, the Parakeet prefers not to ruffle any feathers where appearance is concerned. With fashion help from a girlfriend, he will perhaps exhibit a modicum of style. On the other hand, he might wear what his mom picked out for him, hence those creased, stonewashed jeans and the sweater vest over a turtleneck.

BEHAVIOR: Thoroughly domesticated and agreeable to a fault, the Parakeet truly believes there's no place like home. Rather than drinking with the guys after work, he comes home for dinner every night promptly at 5:30. Generally easy to get along with, he doesn't shirk household chores and is quite "well-trained," mindful of not leaving the toilet seat up or his bed unmade. His greatest wish in life is for the two of you to have your own John Jr. and wee, darling Suzie playing idyllically on the swing-set in the backyard. Like the pet parakeet, Parakeet boys have a cheerful disposition, and may even whistle while they work. He'd make an ideal "Stepford Husband" prototype—might he possibly be descended from Mike Brady?

MATING HABITS: Reliable and consistent, the Parakeet won't stand you up on dates. (He's the type who shows up fifteen minutes early and then circles the 'hood in his car 'till he's five minutes past perfectly punctual.) He'll agree to any activity you've planned but is generally content to curl up with you, a movie rental, and a carton of Chinese takeout—or the "pheasant under glass with a white wine reduction" he can whip up for you in twenty minutes flat.

HABITAT: Existing predominantly in that vast no-man's land of greater suburbia, the Parakeet can be found hanging out at strip malls and chain restaurants frequented by the vast majority of Pigeon boys. More often, however, he'll be grooming his pristine lawn, cleaning the gutters, or perhaps lounging in the common pool area of his apartment complex saying a friendly "hello" to everyone who walks by.

NEST: The Parakeet's nest will have a decidedly domestic aura, decorated in a style just this side of girly with a country kitchen motif or poufy valance curtains chosen for him by mom or a previous girlfriend. Indeed, this is a nest that women feel welcome in, thanks to the fact that he keeps nary a porn mag or *Sports Illustrated* swimsuit issue in sight. In the neatly organized garage, you'll find plenty of tools and other manly tinker toys, as well as a set of golf clubs (for when he plays a round with your dad). A dog of the Lab or Golden Retriever variety is commonplace.

HOW TO LURE: Seeking out a Parakeet can be difficult, since most varieties of the species are normally

The Bird, The Boy

Just as parakeet birds are given mirrors and colorful plastic toys to keep them amused, Parakeet boys are equally delighted by new gadgets for the home, like a Weed Whacker, Bose sound system, or any random offering in the SkyMall catalog.

housebound. Try domestic destinations like Bed Bath & Beyond, garden nurseries, or hardware stores, where you might suggestively ask his advice on how to "locate a stud" or "find a good screw." If you don't see a wedding ring, ask him out. He's so damn agreeable, he'll likely say yes.

FLIGHT PATTERN: Like a pet parakeet that's used to being caged, this boy specimen isn't prone to flying away. Instead, *you'll* probably hit the road when you need a little more adventure than staying in on Friday nights to play Boggle and watch *20/20.* Either that or his constant acquiescence will make you long for the feisty flirtation that comes with any decent Hepburn/Tracy relationship. To put it simply, you'll get pissed off when you realize you *can't* piss him off.

PRIZED FOR: His consistent and predictable presence. Plus the fact that you'll always have a place to do your laundry for free. (Play your cards right and he may even do your laundry for you.)

The Subspecies

Love's Bitch
(*Yesdearium delirium*)

Also known as the Yes Man, Love's Bitch does his girlfriend's bidding no matter how ridiculous the request. He can be found clutching her purse with a plaintive look on his face as she spends forty-five minutes trying on outfits at the mall. He'll get roped into activities like ballroom dance lessons and is expected to give up sporting events or weekly poker nights for mandatory "snuggle time." Everything she says to him is in a nagging, patronizing tone of voice: "Honey, I *told you we're* watching our carbs. Now throw that Pop-Tart away!"

BOY TIP: While Love's Bitch may seem like the perfect accommodating boyfriend, don't be so quick to hunt one up. His lack of spine and inability to stand up for himself can be rather unattractive, unless you're the demanding dominatrix sort.

CHARACTERISTIC SONG: "Anything You Want" by Roy Orbison; "If You Asked Me to" by Celine Dion; "Beast of Burden" by the Rolling Stones.

Mr. Martha
(*Cuisinart domestica*)

Mr. Martha does more than just cook, clean, iron, and own a set of napkin rings that he actually uses.

He's familiar with foods that stump the rest of the civilized world ("Persimmons?" "Rutabagas?") and can identify a sheet's thread count with the mere touch of his hand. He loves to throw long, lavish, yuppified dinner parties using kitchen gadgets like ramekins and microplanes. Continues to rave about the invention of Swiffer dust cloths and is annoyingly knowledgeable about wine.

BOY TIP: Mr. Martha will expect you to keep your own house tidy, but just stick to the basics like making your bed and emptying the trash. He'll compulsively clean the rest anytime he's visiting.

CHARACTERISTIC SONG: "Our House" by Crosby, Stills, Nash and Young; "Little Pink Houses" by John Mellencamp.

Guy Your Mom Loves
(Eddiehaskillum ingratiatum)

This hyper, clean-cut variety of Parakeet has "settling down" written all over him. He probably lives in the neighborhood, attends religious services, addresses your Mom as "ma'am," and has a stable-yet-boring job with guaranteed provider prospects. As his number one fan, your mother's face will light up every time his name is mentioned as she secretly plots the details of your wedding.

BOY TIP: Because your mom digs him, you will consequently have zero attraction for him. This fact will lead to snippy exchanges between you and her, during which you can expect to hear ire-inducing phrases like, "Why can't you just give him a chance?" and "But he's such a *nice boy*!"

CHARACTERISTIC SONG: "The Boy Next Door" by Judy Garland; "Mother's Little Helper" by the Rolling Stones.

Suburban Basement Dweller
(Hobbit-holeus subterraneus)

An evolutionary deviation of the traditional Parakeet, this breed lives in his parents' semirefinished basement, above their garage, or in the RV parked in their backyard. While he claims the living situation is temporary, he makes no efforts to pursue other housing opportunities. His abode features hand-me-down furniture, shag carpeting, and paper-thin walls, hence his harsh whispers to "keep your volume down" during romantic encounters on his twin bed or sleeper sofa.

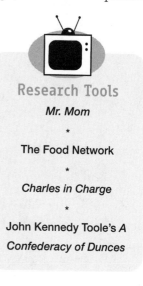

Research Tools

Mr. Mom

∗

The Food Network

∗

Charles in Charge

∗

John Kennedy Toole's *A Confederacy of Dunces*

BOY TIP: Be prepared to endure idle chitchat with his folks whenever you hang out at his place. You'll feel so very "high school" when Lois barges in on the two of you while she's en route to the laundry room. On the bright side, there's never a shortage of decent food.

CHARACTERISTIC SONG: "Mama I'm Coming Home," by Ozzy Osbourne; "In the Basement" by Etta James.

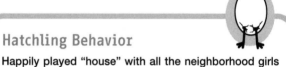

Hatchling Behavior

Happily played "house" with all the neighborhood girls and volunteered to baby-sit their dolls.

❋

Parakeets
and the Women Who Love Them . . .

Does the agreeable "tweet-tweet" of a Parakeet really get your bells and whistles going? Perhaps you're the type of woman who wants a man you can depend on—one who's in tune with your needs and who's up for all that "Your wish is my command" stuff. More likely, you're a simple girl who's fed up with all the games and gimmicks of the modern bachelor. What you really want is someone who has white picket fence—potential and the sense not to go beyond it. If he can get along with your mom (or at least his own), he might just be a contender. Sure, there are some less secure men out there who may mock the Parakeet's deferential demeanor. But as long as he's doing the cooking and cleaning, you'll gladly dub him "master of the house."

*

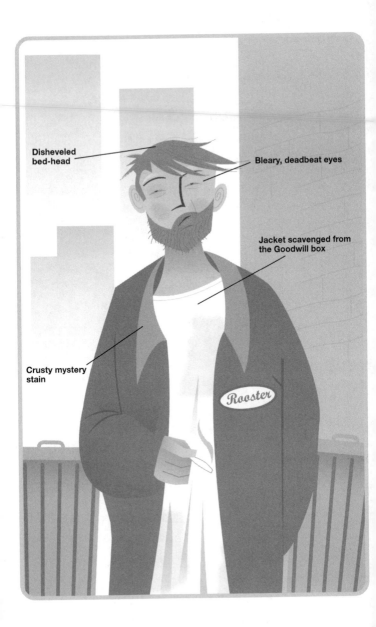

Disheveled bed-head

Bleary, deadbeat eyes

Jacket scavenged from the Goodwill box

Crusty mystery stain

Rooster

12

Fowl

The motivation to dust-bathe remains particularly
strong . . .

—Council of Europe's Recommendation
Concerning Domestic Fowl, adopted by the Standing
Committee on November 28, 1995

In the natural world, "fowl" are the creatures
that wind up on your dinner plate slathered in
BBQ sauce, succulent and tasty. But in the dating
scene, North American Fowl are more stomach-
turning than finger-lickin' good. Even the most am-
ateur boywatchers among us have surely spied,
smelled, or gagged on site at prime specimens of
Fowl, a plentiful breed spanning all socioeconomic
backgrounds from coast to coast. While men of this
category are indeed capable of having many positive attributes, there's no denying that Fowl are the
reason Odor-Eaters, TicTacs, and Wet Naps were
invented.

PLUMAGE: Lacking any innate grooming habits, the Fowl looks like a desert island castaway recently reintroduced to civilization. He sports torn, stained, or sweat-stenched clothing retrieved from mildewy, unlaundered piles in his closet, and his shoes and socks give toxic waste a run for its money so noxious are their fumes. And no, that's not hair gel or pomade in his stringy unkempt locks—it's simply his hair's naturally oily sheen.

BEHAVIOR: Whether he's happily oblivious to the disarray of his own physical condition, engaged in some sort of reacquaintance with his "primal" self, or simply hasn't matured enough to realize that bodily functions are far less humorous than he thinks, the Fowl will gross you out, plain and simple. He rarely washes his hands, burps after drinking expired milk straight from the carton, scratches his groin absentmindedly, and is an unabashed double-dipper when chips and salsa are served. On occasion, he can be spotted "picking a winner" or exiting a bathroom having left "the stable door open and the horse hanging out."

MATING HABITS: Prior to courtship activities, a Fowl feels no compulsion to shower or shave. (By the same token, he won't hold you to any expectation of cleanliness.) On your first date—after clearing a spot for you in his car among the empty two liters of pop and old fast-food takeout bags—he'll take you to a tiny dive restaurant with garish fluorescent lighting and questionable respect for sanitation codes. Once he lands you in the sack, watch out—he might perform the deadly "Dutch Oven."

HABITAT: Seek him out at weeklong rock concerts like Coachella or Burning Man, where he'll afterward camp out in his car in a summer-long tour of U.S. national parks. (As he's not reliant on indoor plumbing, he's well suited to the great outdoors and is particularly undaunted by Port-O-Lets and gas station johns.) In urban areas, he is often mistaken for your garden-variety transient.

NEST: Permeated by a pungent, unrecognizable odor, his dwelling resembles the devastation from old newsreels of the bombing of Dresden. Food-encrusted dishes teeter precariously in the sink and items in his fridge have developed enough fur to merit petting zoo status. Most nightmarish is the bathroom, best entered without focusing one's gaze in any particular direction. Toilet paper is unlikely and bars of soap, if extant, will be petrified and cemented to the sink, rendering them almost unusable. (Try to avoid using his bathroom at any cost, but in emergency "gotta go, gotta go" situations, opt for the public rest room crouch.)

HOW TO LURE: Disregard those trifling Board of Health suggestions and abandon your need for luxury items like clean silverware and dental floss. If you can manage not to flinch when his pet ferret

The Bird, The Boy

Many feathered fowl friend takes pleasure in rolling around on the ground to coat themselves with dirt in a practice known as "dust-bathing." So, too, a Fowl guy feels comfortable forgoing a shower for days on end. (In rare cases, a visible cloud of dust and odor can be seen—think Pigpen of Peanuts' Gang fame.)

poos on your new skirt, you'll win this guy's heart forever.

FLIGHT PATTERN: While delivering his "I'm dumping you" speech, he'll intently study the glob of earwax he's scratched from his inner canal rather than look you in the eye. You'll be so distracted by the crusty mystery stain on his shirt that you'll barely notice you've just been let go. But let's face it: *You'll* probably opt to ditch him first when you can no longer continue to watch him substitute his own shirtsleeve for the task Kleenex was so aptly invented for.

PRIZED FOR: Not only does he get along famously with your prepubescent little brother, he also won't hog the bathroom, as he has no preening of his own to attend to.

The Subspecies

Blissfully Unhygienic Guy
(Oblivious hygienicus)

As his name implies, it never dawns on Blissfully Unhygienic Guy that his general disinterest in attending to his own physical condition is a turnoff for others. Whether he's unaware of his chronic halitosis, hasn't changed his bed sheets since May of 2003, or simply feels there's nothing wrong with turning his boxer shorts inside out for a second day's use, he's the type of guy Mr. Clean would love to give a good ass-whoopin'.

BOY TIP: Learn to compromise. While you may convince him to wear a clean shirt and tie to your company Christmas party, he'll still insist on wearing the gym shoes that are so old they're held together by twine.

CHARACTERISTIC SONG: "That Smell" by Lynyrd Skynyrd; "Dirrty" by Christina Aguilera.

The Purposeful Grotesque
(Deliberatum bawdyium)

Never having progressed beyond the emotional maturity of a seven-year-old, the Purposeful Grotesque will try to weird you out by turning his eyelids inside out, bending back his double-jointed thumb, or belching the alphabet. While visiting zoos, he gets a tremendous kick out of watching animals copulate. On speaking, he averages 2.4 expletives in every sentence he utters and has developed a significant lexicon of tawdry terms for intercourse (e.g., "doing the tube steak boogie").

BOY TIP: Look for this breed en masse at Farrelly brothers' movies.

CHARACTERISTIC SONG: "Beans, beans, the musical fruit . . ."

As Seen In Nature

Puck from *The Real World*, San Francisco

*

The blokes from *Trainspotting*

*

Nick Nolte

*

Mickey Rourke

*

Bart Simpson

Grody Au Natural
(Treehuggerum nastium)

An environmentalist and lover of the Great Outdoors, the Grody Au Natural doesn't believe in hygiene beyond what Mother Nature provides. He's often bearded, bathes infrequently (to conserve water), and rejects most disinfectants and cleansers (including deodorant, sadly). His bathroom features a sign taped above the toilet: "If it's yellow, let it mellow, if it's brown, flush it down." On the bright side, once you're dating the Grody Au Natural, feel free to stop shaving your armpits.

BOY TIP: Lure this breed by slapping a Jerry Bear sticker on your car bumper and offering him a ride when he's hitching to the next Phish concert.

CHARACTERISTIC SONG: Anything by the Nitty Gritty Dirt Band; "You Never Wash Up After Yourself" by Radiohead.

※

Fowl
and the Women Who Love Them . . .

If you can tolerate bad odors and squalid living conditions in the name of love, congratulations—you're a better woman than most. In tune with humanity's most base and natural state, you're easygoing, have a resolute stomach, and generally aren't put off by bodily fluid (e.g., pee on the toilet seat). Inner beauty is what matters most to you, even when the outside package is a far cry from pristine. (Beauty and the Beast comes to mind if the Beast resided at the city dump, refused to bathe, and never seemed likely to mutate into a prince.) Either you're very broad-minded or, dare we say, you might simply be a Stinky Miss Messy who likes to stick with her own kind.

※

13

Crows

The crows would gather on the railing at the other end
and talk about me . . . they would sit there, in the most
unabashed way, and talk about my clothes, and my hair,
and my complexion, and probable character and voca-
tion and politics . . .

—Mark Twain, *Following the Equator*

The term "as the crow flies" generally implies
the quickest distance between point A and
point B. Yet in conversation, Crow boys take a
more circuitous route—if they succeed in making
a point at all. Like their loudmouth bird counterparts (whose "Caw! Caw!" can truly only be toler-
ated by witches and the evil divas in animated
Disney flicks), the loquacious Crow is never at a loss
for words. Apparently oblivious to that axiom about
silence being golden, he'll talk you into a coma
with his rambling stories and mind-numbing
chitchat. While scarecrows or concrete owls may
keep the feathered crow far afield from farmers'
crops, women of the dating world have no such

preventive tactics at their disposal once they've become a Crow boy's captive audience. At that point, no prayers in the world will get him to shoo.

PLUMAGE: A Crow's appearance is generally not worth mentioning, yet rest assured, his look will prompt a tedious story, be it his odyssey to find the right size sweater at three different J. Crew locations (drawn out for twenty-three minutes in the telling) or the stunning revelation that his barber also cuts the hair of David Letterman's neighbor's stepbrother (an anecdote you've heard at least twice before).

BEHAVIOR: Blessed (or cursed) with the gift for gab, the Crow is comfortable striking up a conversation with just about anyone, from strangers waiting in line at the supermarket ("Ah, Bagel Bites—good choice!") to fellow airplane passengers clearly hoping to spend their four-hour flight absorbed in a book—not the Crow's life story. When engaging in dialogue, the Crow pretends to listen by repeating a frenzied, "uh-huh, uh-huh," clearly anxious to reclaim command of the conversation. His meandering anecdotes take forever to reach a climax, punch line, or denouement—if they get there at all. He's also much given to gossip, which he fails to keep to a respectable low murmur.

MATING HABITS: During courtship, phone conversations with a Crow will go on for hours, though you won't get a word in edgewise apart from monosyllabic interjections like "Wow!" or "Hmm." On the bright side, you'll never have to endure those awkward silences that could lead you to doubt your compatibility. Once you've achieved couple status, a Crow will constantly instigate "State of the Union" addresses, longing to discuss every nuance of your relationship. ("But are you *really* happy sleeping on the left side of the bed?")

HABITAT: The ubiquitous Crow is most noticeable at establishments where his verbiage stands out: libraries, houses of worship, chamber music concerts, and scholarly lectures, during which a Crow will repeatedly raise his hand to interrupt the speaker with annoyingly tangential questions. Other hangouts include karaoke bars (where he's on the mic) and hovering near the office watercooler, eager to dish the latest dirt. ("Hey, I heard the new secretary used to be a stripper!")

NEST: The Crow's sanctuary is a repository for plenty of conversation pieces, for which he has nauseatingly long stories. (We'll spare you further details, but rest assured—he won't.) A novelty singing trout may exist in a high-traffic area of his home, startling you every time you set off its motion sensor. He'll also have a television or stereo blaring at all times.

HOW TO LURE: Lend him your ear, appear fascinated by his stories, and flatter him with comparisons to ancient orators. (Think Virgil, Cicero, or Andy Rooney.) When you simply must end his droning monologue, interrupt him midsentence by commencing "Operation: Makeout Session." Plant your lips on his and try not to come up for air.

FLIGHT PATTERN: He'll dump you with the ironic criticism, "I feel like we're not communicating."

PRIZED FOR: His ability to converse with anyone, from your mother to your postman to your catatonic grandfather in a nursing home. As a future dad, he'll tell terrific bedtime stories that will send the kids to the land of nod within minutes.

The Subspecies

The Baron of Boring
(Yoomaykme yawnium)

Exhibiting a monotone voice ("Buellerrrrr . . . Buellerrrrr"), the Baron of Boring will expound upon topics that no one could conceivably care about, be it the minutiae of military regiments in the Franco-Prussian War or the finer points of metallurgy. He enjoys "spinning yarns" (his words) and may do a play-by-play review of an NFL game, a page-by-page recap of a Tolstoy novel, or a second-by-second narrative of a *Saturday Night Live* skit.

BOY TIP: His "That reminds me of a time" segues are never relevant, so learn to endure these narrations by maintaining an interested "I'm listening" look on your face while you happily space out or make mental to-do lists.

CHARACTERISTIC SONG: "Don't Speak" by No Doubt, but not Depeche Mode's "Enjoy the Silence."

The Prince of PR
(Networkus jabberjawnium)

Born to excel in the world of politics or publicity, the Prince of PR has an answer for everything, even if he has to make something up. Also known as the Bullshit Artiste, the Prince of PR spends every moment touting his driving cause and trying to convince others to accept his party line. He may throw out hefty vocab words like "commensurate" and "predicated" to make his euphemisms and double-talk sound more palatable. He didn't "have an affair," after all—he had a "semi-infidelitous dalliance."

BOY TIP: Since he likes stories that have a happy ending, the Prince of PR is adroit at glossing over historical facts. The corralling of Native Americans onto small Western reservations in the nineteenth century is, for him, a "facilitation for the future of Indian gaming. . . . We basically handed those tribes their own shot at Vegas!"

CHARACTERISTIC SONG: "You Spin Me Round (Like a Record)" by Dead or Alive; "Ac-cent-tchu-ate the Positive" by Bing Crosby.

Dad Guy
(Hoos yourdaddium)

Identified by his bad jokes and lame advice, Dad Guy has slightly troubling views on race relations and "alternative lifestyles," couched in the guise of dunderheaded dadness. He may sport a premature beer belly and is legendary for ridiculous proclamations that highlight his out-of-touch dorkiness: "Well, if I'm in California, I'd better get my ear pierced!"

BOY TIP: Save yourself from some annoying lectures by remembering to get your oil changed regularly and read with sufficient lighting. Just don't forget to turn off those lights when you leave the room. ("Electricity doesn't grow on trees, you know!")

CHARACTERISTIC SONG: "Papa Don't Preach" by Madonna; "Father Figure" by George Michael.

Mr. Megaphone
(Decibel obnoxium)

As his name implies, Mr. Megaphone is known for a lack of volume control that's sadly demonstrated in public places. Whether he's blurting out commentary in movie theaters ("Someone told me that guy's the killer!") or broadcasting his embarrassingly personal cell phone conversations ("Mom, I told her about my rash! Chill!"), Mr. Megaphone will have you speaking in a whisper as you desperately try to compensate for his booming projection.

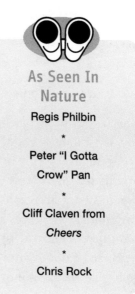

As Seen In Nature

Regis Philbin

*

Peter "I Gotta Crow" Pan

*

Cliff Claven from *Cheers*

*

Chris Rock

BOY TIP: His liberal use of expletives in family restaurants may have you shamefaced as outraged soccer moms dart you angry glances. Still, you'll

Grub

Pops gum, slurps his soup, and chomps noisily on apples and Cracker Jacks.

never lose track of Mr. Megaphone at a party or crowded rock concert, and his decibel level could be a lifesaver if the two of you ever get lost in the woods.

CHARACTERISTIC SONG: "Shout" by Tears For Fears; "Voices Carry" by 'Til Tuesday.

✳

Crows

and the Women Who Love Them . . .

Chatty Kathys may think themselves perfectly suited to date a Crow, but in actuality only quiet types can ever really offset the constant yammering of this talkative breed. Although the bird in question has long been considered an omen of bad luck, any woman who loves a Crow boy can clearly recognize the benefits of his outspokenness. You'll never *ever* need to offer him a penny for his thoughts—he'll give them free of charge. Plus, there's something comfortably lulling about the din of his one-man dialogue, much the same way some people need the TV on to fall asleep. A group of caterwauling ravens (members of the crow family) roost at the Tower of London, and the English believe the

British Empire will fall should those garrulous birds ever depart. In the same way, once you've grown accustomed to your guy's familiar squawking, you may find yourself hard pressed to live without him. So if that little voice in your ear says "He's a keeper," you'll know it's right. Just bear in mind that the voice in your ear is probably his.

✳

14

Chickens

I had before heard that he was a poor-spirited creature;
but on this occasion, I couldn't help seeing that he was
as frightened as a chicken in a bundle of hemp.
 —Alessandro Manzoni, *I Promessi Sposi*

You'll get tired of chickens. . . .
 —Tom Cruise, *Interview With A Vampire*

Ever since Chicken Little ran around town
spouting Doomsday histrionics, there has ex-
isted a category of men with similar pee-in-
their-pants apprehension and fear when it comes to
approaching the opposite sex—or life in general.
While it's easy to be drawn to their sensitivity and
pacifying personalities, the yellow-bellied nature of
Chickens can be difficult to get past. Whether it's the
scrawny man at the beach who gets sand kicked in
his face, the trembling fellow scared of spiders, or
the guy on *The Price Is Right* who can't seem to spin

the bonus wheel one full rotation, these wimps and weaklings make the Cowardly Lion look like a rabid killing machine.

PLUMAGE: Scrawny and thin, most Chickens generally aren't flashy in their dress or demeanor, and are completely petrified at the prospect of trying a new look. If a Chicken dares to buy a pale yellow dress shirt instead of his standard white, this risky leap into the world of color will probably remain in the closet, tags intact. Trips to the barber cause particular alarm, as he's sure his new 'do looks like a woman's haircut (even though the outside observer doesn't notice any difference).

BEHAVIOR: Chickens are in a perpetual state of worry and fret, and the sources are myriad: the eerie calliope music of ice cream trucks, overzealous telemarketers, Gap employees, being stalked by hook-armed killers on country roads at night, or getting locked in a Waffle House rest room. Highly informed about a variety of disease symptoms and worst-case scenarios, Chickens are happy to share their panic with anyone who will listen, persuading you to invest in carpal tunnel wrist guards as well as a gas mask for your poodle. Physically and emotionally, they're hardly a stalwart breed: Drinking even one Michelob Light gives most Chickens a "major buzz," and any illness-themed movie (*Terms of Endearment, Love Story*) will render them teary-eyed and useless for the rest of the evening.

MATING HABITS: When it comes time to ask someone out on a date, Chickens enter a state of heightened anxiety (orange alert!) and have been known to script phone calls as preparation for asking someone out. (Expect several hang-ups before he makes actual contact, and then much throat-clearing and stammering when he's trying to get to the point.) Once in a relationship, the sensitive Chicken boy needs regular reassurance of your love, constantly asking for hugs when you're clearly otherwise occupied putting in contact lenses or balancing your checkbook.

HABITAT: With the Chicken, the question is not so much where he is as where he isn't. That list includes thrill rides at amusement parks, exotic vacation destinations where the potential is high for getting dismembered by a shark or catching West Nile virus, and Army recruitment centers. It's safe to say that Chickens are drawn to spaces where their sensitivity will be nurtured and extolled, e.g. Women's Studies classes and candlelight vigils.

NEST: With smoke and carbon monoxide detectors in every room, a generously stocked medicine cabinet (complete with an Anthrax vaccine), and multiple deadbolts on the outside doors, a Chicken's nest is more secure than a bomb shelter, as well as completely childproof. (Don't mistake this concern for fatherly intent; he's not a fan of "small children and their germs.") Rest assured that his home doesn't

The Bird, The Boy

Real-life chickens are fussy eaters, turning their beaks up at bitter food. Chicken boys are equally finicky, refusing to try even just one bite of exotic cuisine, whether it's sushi ("Don't even get me started on the health risks"), Ethiopian ("The bread is like spongy skin"), or Peruvian ("It gives me digestive woe").

straddle a fault line, and is well-stocked with bottled water, canned goods, and duct tape.

HOW TO LURE: Getting a date with a Chicken requires a bit of effort on your part. Although most are hesitant to make the first move, they won't turn down the advances of an assertive female. Be gentle and encouraging, as if you're approaching an orphaned baby rabbit. If you really want to boost his confidence, act similarly nervous and feign a stutter.

FLIGHT PATTERN: Things will get serious, and he'll freak out. (Or, he'll watch a *Dateline* special about obsessive girlfriend stalkers, and he'll freak out.) Too cowardly to dump you in person, he'll do it via e-mail or voicemail . . . or he might just avoid you altogether by going MIA, getting Caller ID, and "not being home" when you happen to call.

PRIZED FOR: His lack of testosterone-motivated bravery and machismo can be seen as a bold defiance of all-too-predictable gender conventions. That, and once he's actually dating someone, he's way too bashful to cheat.

The Subspecies

The First-Move 'Fraidy Cat
(Tootimid tutoucherum)

While his sex drive is as fully functioning as any other male's, the First-Move 'Fraidy Cat is crippled with fear and intimidation when it comes to sealing the deal, so to speak. Merely being in the presence of an object of his affection will elicit habitual hand-wringing, a nervous eye tick, and sweaty palms. 'Fraidy Cats often flock together on weekend nights to play poker games and other all-male activities, while collectively bemoaning the lack of decent chicks as a way to mask their own cowardice.

BOY TIP: When it comes to dropping you off at the end of a first date, the Fraidy Cat will preempt the anxiety-provoking goodnight kiss by letting you out on the curb in the middle of a busy intersection as if he were executing a D-Day drop-off on the beaches of Normandy.

CHARACTERISTIC SONG: "Too Shy" by Kajagoogoo; "Let's Wait a While" by Janet Jackson.

Mr. Sensitive
(*Kleenex usurpius*)

Mr. Sensitive cries at the drop of a hat—over Hallmark commercials, news stories about beached whales, any movie starring Hume Cronyn and/or Jessica Tandy, and after sex—so moved is he by the shared intimacy. In his nest, you'll find more candles than a Pottery Barn, the occasional Native American "dream catcher," a poster of Gustav Klimt's *The Kiss*, and a collection of *Chicken Soup for the Soul* books.

BOY TIP: On breaking up, he'll tell you you're cold and heartless and he can't continue in such an emotional vacuum of a relationship; then he'll curl up in a fetal position in his closet and sob for three days.

As Seen In Nature

Frodo Baggins

*

Sesame Street's **Grover**

*

Pony Boy from
The Outsiders

*

Smithers from
The Simpsons

CHARACTERISTIC SONG: "Everybody Hurts" by REM; "Vincent" by Don McLean.

Cried for days when Bambi's mother died and wouldn't let go of his mom's hand after seeing *Dumbo*.

The Sissy Boy
(Lackingium testosteronium)

The Sissy Boy—also known as He Who Speaks Softly and Runs Like a Girl—doesn't know how to change a tire, let alone change the oil in his car, and is still haunted by humiliations he suffered in junior high Phys Ed. In a Dickens novel, he'd be the kindly but pallid male heir wasting away beneath a flannel blanket. ("'Do not sorrow when I am gone,' he said in a soft, lilting voice.") Hardware stores make him nervous.

BOY TIP: In "fight or flight" situations, he'll choose flight every time, so prepare to fend for yourself when confronted with a flasher or accosted by rude hooligans.

CHARACTERISTIC SONG: "Coward of the County" by Kenny Rogers.

※

Chickens
and the Women Who Love Them . . .

Think manly men are a bit overrated? Would you rather drop dead than date the mustachioed gentleman on the Brawny paper towels package? If you answered yes to either of these questions, you may be a good match for a Chicken. After all, you've never needed your boyfriend to do double duty as your beast of burden (hauling boxes, stamping out roaches), and daring feats of heroic chivalry are a tad too medieval for your taste. In fact, you prefer a guy who's sweet, sensitive, and yes, even a little bit shy. Whether you're the mothering type or simply like being the assertive one in the relationship, you see strengths in this type where the rest of society only finds weakness. Put it this way: You'd gladly cross the road to get to his side.

※

Bizarre Bird Fact

Chickens haven't always been associated with cowardice. The Romans viewed the chicken as a sacred symbol of bravery, and dedicated it to Mars, the god of war. They trained the birds to fight like gladiators, feeding them garlic to increase their courage and ferocity. Every Roman army had its own flock of chickens, which commanders used to help determine whether or not they should go into battle.

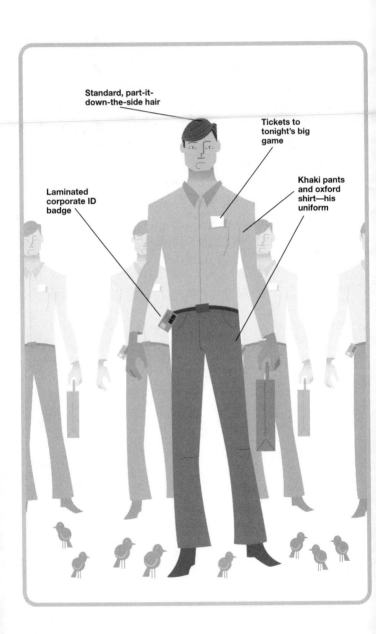

Standard, part-it-down-the-side hair

Tickets to tonight's big game

Khaki pants and oxford shirt—his uniform

Laminated corporate ID badge

15

Pigeons

Pigeons marry just like people and stay that way until
one of them dies.

—Marlon Brando, *On the Waterfront*

Woody Allen called pigeons "rats with
wings," and while it's true that cities in
America are inundated with these non-
descript feathered multitudes, they shouldn't be
summarily branded as pests. Smart and docile,
they've been helpmates to humans for centuries, but
since they lack the flashy showmanship of other
birds (and can hardly be considered rare), they generally don't attract much praise or attention. Pigeon
boys, too, are scattered across every square inch of
this great nation, though you may never give these
Average Joes a second glance. Yet what they lack in
the "Wow!" factor, Pigeons certainly make up for in
steadfastness and dependability. Some may reject
this breed as far too boring to be boyfriend worthy,
but many others have forged a happy, lifelong bond

with a practical Pigeon. So before you totally rule out a future with a Pigeon, why not at least throw him a few crumbs? He may just surprise you.

PLUMAGE: Dressed in the mass-produced uniforms of national chain retailers (The Gap, Abercrombie & Fitch, Tommy Hilfiger, and American Eagle Outfitters), this everyman is generally inoffensive to the eye, though he would never be classified as exceedingly handsome. He owns one suit for job interviews and funerals, and his work attire consists of khaki pants and a white (or light blue) oxford shirt or crewneck sweater. Whether mousy brown or dishwater blond, his clean-cut coif gets routine maintenance with a quick jaunt to Great Clips every month.

BEHAVIOR: Pigeons love reading John Grisham, watching James Bond, drinking domestic beer, and staring blankly for hours at ESPN. After graduating from State U. with a business degree, he now works in a vague career like consulting or accounts receivable, clocking eight-hour days in some dreary industrial park. After hours, the Pigeon sticks to a general routine, attending both the golf course and religious services once a week. Though he's generally not a risk taker, he will gladly partake in "safe" adventures (bungee jumping at tourist Meccas like Cancun: Crayyyzzzyyy!). He shies away from having any real point of view on controversial subjects and prefers to roost on fences or in the middle of the road, metaphorically speaking.

MATING HABITS: Don't expect love at first sight, given that your first encounter with a Pigeon will probably include banal edifying questions ("Where are you from?" "What do you do?"). Like a real-life pigeon, which feeds its mate as part of the courtship ritual, Pigeon boys will plan the standard default date: dinner and a movie. (Don't suggest an indie flick, as he prefers blockbusters featuring the Toms: Cruise or Hanks.) Conversation is neither gripping nor hilarious and will likely involve a lot of general and obvious declarations: "If there's one thing I hate, it's people who hurt kids." In the first few weeks of dating, you'll totally forget what your Pigeon's face looks like in between dates and will experience an "Oh yeah" moment of recognition each time you meet up. While he is not bred to offer outpourings of heartfelt emotion, he does share more subtle proof of his affections, like calling when he says he will or offering up the vulnerable admission: "I had fun. You're pretty cool."

HABITAT: Ubiquitous in society, Pigeons (both the bird and boy) generally remain in the vicinity of where they were born, never venturing far from their original nest. From Monday through Friday, the Pigeon boy earns a middling wage, while on weekends, he can be found in line at cineplexes, walking the mall ("Hey! They have a Banana Republic here!"), or enjoying a Bloomin' Onion at chain restaurants like T.G.I.Friday's or Chili's.

NEST: Furnished with a light-colored wood furniture suite, a Pigeon's nest has a neutral color scheme (think "oatmeal" and "buff"). Mass-produced prints by Ansel Adams spruce up the walls, and the Pigeon owns every must-have electronic gadget once it goes on sale at Best Buy. The mailman never seems to deliver anything of interest besides bills and junk mail for "occupant."

HOW TO LURE: Like their bird counterparts, if you feed the Pigeon boy, he will come. Make him cookies or invite him over for dinner, and once you've got him pecking at your feet, don't scare him off by doing anything too unconventional. Sudden moves like piercing your eyebrow or quitting your job to read tarot cards for a living will prompt him to flutter away in a tizzy.

FLIGHT PATTERN: In the same way that cities import peregrine falcons to "take care" of their feral pigeon problem, you'll ditch your bland beau when you meet a non-Pigeon who can offer more in the way of excitement. Within three months, you'll have a hard time remembering your ex-Pigeon's name and will think back on him as "that nice guy."

PRIZED FOR: Being highly parent-friendly. Hoping for a future son-in-law, Sid and Trudy will beam with joy every time you mention your Pigeon, and they'll never question your actions so long as he's involved. ("No daughter of ours is going to invest in some crazy pyramid scheme . . . Oh, *Douggg* told you about it? Well then, sign us up, too!")

The Subspecies

The Sports Fan
(ESPNonymous vicarious)

Whether he's migrating to the local sports arena on a seasonal basis or nesting in front of the TV each weekend and Monday night, the Sports Fan fixates on athletic events with other Pigeon multitudes. While he lacks the bobbing head gesture of his feathered counterpart, he responds innately to "The Wave" every times it passes through his seating section. He loves fantasy leagues and betting pools, but unlike the true fanatic who paints his entire head and torso in the team colors, the Sports Fan sticks to wearing a basic team jersey or ball cap. (He's a Pigeon, after all—not a freak.)

BOY TIP: Be prepared to plan your relationship's schedule around the Superbowl, March Madness, or the Cubs' home games. If your sister's wedding coincides with a big prizefight, he'll send his regrets. ("This might not be her only wedding but this is definitely my only chance to see Lennox Lewis ringside!")

CHARACTERISTIC SONG: "We Are the Champions" by Queen and, of course, his college fight song.

The BSK (Blue Shirt and Khakis)
(Dimeadozen indiscriminatum)

Sporting the classic look of a Land's End catalog model, the BSK is the reason Polo shirts will never go out of style. Their names are as commonplace as their demeanor (Bill, Dan, Jim, Rob . . .) and many pursue careers in engineering, computer programming, or accounting. In hot pursuit of the American Dream (2.5 kids and all that jazz), he'll likely drive a safe, affordable, and fuel-efficient sedan like the Honda Accord or Saturn Eclipse. The BSK will never blow a paycheck in Vegas or call in sick to work when he's not. At his most daring, he may experiment with growing a goatee.

BOY TIP: If you're planning a future with a BSK, expect to reside in an upscale tract home of a planned community named "Vista Glen Estates" or "Briarly Creek," which will be located a respectable distance from any unsavory urban centers.

CHARACTERISTIC SONG: "Ants Go Marching" by Dave Matthews; "I Feel Like a Number" by Bob Seeger.

Middle Management Man
(401kadium dilbertium)

A cog in the wheel of some ginormous corporation, Middle Management Man spends much of the day within a flimsy cubicle under fluorescent lights that give his face a deathly pallor. This diligent worker deserves a raise but is unlikely to ask for one, preferring instead to passively wait for his meager yearly cost of living adjustment. After ten years on the job, his own boss still calls him Brett instead of Brad. He's not cut out for commission-based jobs as he lacks the networking skills and sales savvy of other, more cutthroat businessmen.

Grub

Iceberg lettuce, cheese pizza, white bread, vanilla ice cream, and bottled Bud.

BOY TIP: Given that he's usually pushing paper and watching the clock, he'll expect you to keep him amused throughout the day with forwarded e-mail jokes and the like since they're his only escape from the daily grind.

CHARACTERISTIC SONG: "Nine to Five" by Dolly Parton; "Morning Train" by Sheena Easton.

Hatchling Behavior

In school, Pigeons were neither the geeks nor the popular kids, earning countless "participation" ribbons and awards for perfect attendance.

❋

Pigeons
and the Women Who Love Them . . .

Cities spend hundreds of thousands of dollars each year to clean caustic pigeon droppings from municipal buildings, public statues, and the like. Pigeon boys, on the other hand, are fairly harmless, which is why you may find yourself dating a member of this boy breed more often than not. You've probably already jumped aboard the Pigeon bandwagon if you like a man with dependability and a sound, structured life—one who won't intimidate, embarrass, or burden you with the cumbersome issues of a more colorful, impassioned (or flaky) personality. Perhaps you're the type of girl whose life is ruined when your favorite shampoo is out of stock or your favorite restaurant goes belly up. In that case, the Pigeon is your perfect match: Not only is he completely predictable, but if he flies the coop there will forever be twenty more to fill his shoes.

❋

Research Tools

Office Space

*

Diary of a Nobody
by George and Weedon
Grossmith

*

ESPN

*

Brave New World by
Aldous Huxley

*

Jude the Obscure by
Thomas Hardy

*

Suburbia

*

The Invisible Man by
H. G. Wells

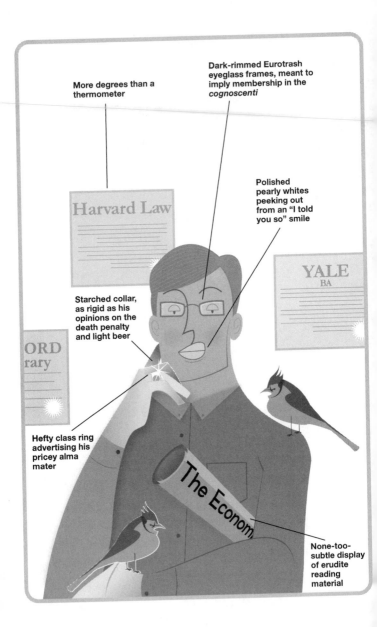

More degrees than a thermometer

Dark-rimmed Eurotrash eyeglass frames, meant to imply membership in the *cognoscenti*

Polished pearly whites peeking out from an "I told you so" smile

Harvard Law

YALE
BA

Starched collar, as rigid as his opinions on the death penalty and light beer

ORD
rary

Hefty class ring advertising his pricey alma mater

The Econom

None-too-subtle display of erudite reading material

16

Blue Jays

All jays make their share of noise in the world; they fret and scold about trifles, quarrel over anything, and keep everything in a ferment when they are about.
—Elliot Coues, *Birds of the Northwest*

A jay hasn't got any more principle than a Congressman.
—Mark Twain, *A Tramp Abroad*

Beneath the blue jay's bright feathers and dignified crest lies an attitude in dire need of adjustment. Perpetually hot under the collar, jays defend their territory with vigor and throw nasty fits whenever they feel threatened. Smaller birds scatter with fright in their presence, leaving these mobsters to monopolize backyard birdfeeders. An equally contentious bunch, Blue Jay boys are just as headstrong and argumentative. Forever aspiring to get the best seat, the final word, or the last laugh, this uber-competitive type won't ever win first place in a congeniality contest—but he'll sure as heck die trying.

PLUMAGE: Best recognized by his sulky defensive stance and pouting puss, a Blue Jay manifests an aura of perturbed arrogance that's impossible to miss. He rarely dresses down, preferring crisp, button-up shirts with collars so starched they could stand by themselves. On weekends he dons his college class ring or alumni sweatshirt as a not-so-subtle reminder of his cerebral pedigree. In times of intensified hostility, you can spot a Blue Jay shooting "the bird" (no pun intended), a universal gesture among this breed.

BEHAVIOR: A Blue Jay's sole purpose in life seems to be proving others wrong. "My mistake" isn't in his lexicon, though you'll hear some variation of "I told you so" on a near daily basis. Forever on the defense, Blue Jays frequently mistake commonplace remarks for biting insults, thus feeling instantly victimized. ("Yes, that Jon Stewart *is* a funny guy—and I'm not?") If you listen closely in the wild, you might hear his signature call, which he utters in a hostile pitch: *"What are you implyingggg? What are you implyingggg?"*

MATING HABITS: A Blue Jay is particularly argumentative in the company of females, as he's loath to admit that a girl may know more than he does. Yet curiously, this defensive breed has a latent sense of inadequacy that hinders his ability to find a mate. Don't be surprised if he asks you out in a back-handed and slightly hostile fashion: "I would have asked you to dinner, but I figured you'd probably have said no anyway."

HABITAT: Blue Jays make excellent candidates for the law profession and are usually seen flocking around courtrooms. Their distinctive call is also heard on talk radio, where they love to offer up their two cents regarding the charlatans in Washington or the injustices of the federal income tax.

NEST: So far, concrete data is limited. Because the Blue Jay doesn't like to have his nest scrutinized (not to mention he doesn't want people "casing the joint"), few people are permitted to enter. What we know from firsthand accounts, however, is that Blue Jays own multiple reference books to quickly settle any argument about, say, the current president of Brazil or who invented the zipper.

HOW TO LURE: Treat him like the know-it-all he thinks he is. Casually mention that he'd make a great contestant on *Jeopardy*, then challenge him to any sort of game or competition and purposefully lose. It will feed his ego and he'll love you for it. When offering him compliments, express them in a way that could not possibly be considered backhanded. Or adopt the stance of a deaf-mute—the less you say, the less he can take the wrong way.

FLIGHT PATTERN: When you get miffed at him for correcting you on the pronunciation of Coeur d'Alene,

> ### The Bird, The Boy
> Just as blue jays in the wilderness can imitate the call of hawks to freak out their feathered foes, a Blue Jay boy likes to pretend he's more of a badass than he actually is. However, when he asks a potential rival in a barroom brawl to "step outside" with him, the Jay will end up getting his butt kicked nine times out of ten.

he'll tell you you're completely inflexible and that he can't have a future with someone so resistant to constructive criticism. (Breaking up with you first is the Blue Jay's ultimate defense mechanism, as he'd rather dump you before you beat him to the chase.)

PRIZED FOR: His type-A personality. Although his perfectionism can be annoying, it can also come in handy—like when he's buying you a diamond.

The Subspecies

Contrary Larry
(Boy bellicosus)

Known for flip-flopping his opinions at any given moment, Contrary Larry would argue with a turnip if given the chance. A true champion in the art of ranting and/or raving, he will have selective amnesia about conversations you may have had only a week prior, then will angrily accuse you of putting words in his mouth. Take the liberty of ordering him a Coke (his soda of choice for as long as you've known him) and he'll swear his delicate taste buds can only tolerate Pepsi. He may use linguistic gymnastics to win an argument, as in "That depends on what the meaning of the word *is* is."

BOY TIP: Contrary Larry sticks to his guns so adamantly that he can succeed in making you doubt heretofore unquestioned truths, like the fact that the Earth is round. If you want to quickly wrap up an exasperating argument, simply leave your ego at the door and murmur, "You're right. So very right."

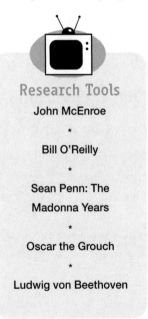

Research Tools

John McEnroe

*

Bill O'Reilly

*

Sean Penn: The Madonna Years

*

Oscar the Grouch

*

Ludwig von Beethoven

CHARACTERISTIC SONG: Gershwin's "Let's Call the Whole Thing Off" ("You say 'to-may-to,' I say 'to-mah-to' . . ."); "Hello, Good-bye" by the Beatles.

Defensive Guy
(Blameus resisticus)

Wearing a metaphorical flak jacket, Defensive Guy deciphers any benign comment as a caustic personal attack. "Please pass the salt" somehow translates to an insult on his cooking abilities, and if you tell him he's got a nice smile, he'll immediately assume you're poking fun at his slightly crooked bicuspids. Subscribing to the "Whatyoutalkin'bout, Willis?" philosophy of life, he constantly suspects that people are out to undermine him.

BOY TIP: Defensive Guy occasionally busts himself by getting defensive over things prematurely, thus tipping you off to his guilt: "Before you go pointing fingers, *it wasn't me* who spilled coffee on page 63 of your diary!"

CHARACTERISTIC SONG: "I'm Not Responsible" by Tom Jones; "It Ain't Me, Babe" by Bob Dylan.

One-Upmanship Guy

(Autonomous horntrumpetus)

With his chin held high and chest puffed out, One-Upmanship Guy struts around trying to claim first place in intelligence, athletics, wit, or even who gets the last Oreo. He's not above cheating to win and will resort to clever tactics to ensure victory, like having to go to the bathroom during the middle of a

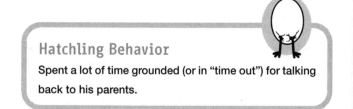

Hatchling Behavior

Spent a lot of time grounded (or in "time out") for talking back to his parents.

Trivial Pursuit question, during which he dials his dad on the cell phone to verify the answer.

BOY TIP: Don't go on dates that could turn competitive. Even miniature golf with this boy can get intensely heated, and a game of Monopoly will mutate into World War III. "Ahem . . . I believe I own those two hotels on Park Place, *so pay up, loser!*"

CHARACTERISTIC SONG: The classic showtune, "Anything You Can Do (I Can Do Better)"; "Big Shot" by Billy Joel.

※

Blue Jays
and the Women Who Love Them . . .

If you're smitten with a Blue Jay, you're up for a good spat every now and then. After all, you probably get off on the sexual tension that comes from a feisty argument. In general, you're a strong-minded thinker who can hold your own during a good debate. Yet in those instances where your guy's feathers are unnecessarily ruffled, you can be a calming force in his life. (Think Hepburn and Fonda in *On Golden Pond.*) Some would say the sparks that come from dating a Blue Jay are worth all the hassles and hissy-fits. But if you welcome him into your bed, just remember: Nine of ten times, he'll wake up on the wrong side of it.

※

Fruity drink laden with novelty props

Head jauntily tossed back in a dramatic laugh

Tuxedo shirt, worn with ironic whimsy on Casual Fridays

Pinstriped "party pants"

Footloose and fancy-free in Beatle boots

17

Flamingos

In Florida consider the flamingo,
Its color passion but its neck a question.
                    —Robert Penn Warren, *Pursuit*

Male flamingos are slightly larger than females, weigh-
ing more and having longer wingspans; however, visual
sex determinations of flamingos are unreliable.
    —Sea World Education Department Resource

Flamingos. There's something peculiar about a
Day-Glo pink bird who stands gingerly on one
spindly leg and hangs out a lot in Miami. In
the same way, there exists a subset of North American males who are similarly eccentric, skirting the
margins of traditional manliness with their eyebrow-
raising approach to life. Never ones to blend in with
the crowd, Flamingos will surely capture your attention, if not your heart. Above all else, they'll definitely add some color to your world.

PLUMAGE: A Flamingo's attire sets him instantly apart from his surroundings as he cultivates a signature look that prompts onlookers to whisper, "Oh my God . . . check *him* out." Look for garb that's seemingly inconsistent with what the rest of humanity is wearing (rainbow suspenders, a Fedora, wool serape, or Capezio jazz shoes). He flashes blindingly white teeth in an ever-present, often completely uncalled-for smile, and his hairstyle may range from "light socket" crazy to a product-laden pompadour.

BEHAVIOR: Life is one big metaphorical song-and-dance number for a Flamingo boy, who seems somehow oblivious to any of the world's harsh and depressing realities. He'll follow his whims wherever they may lead, be it turning his back deck into a tiki lounge or enrolling in a puppeteering apprenticeship on *Sesame Street*. A Flamingo is way too busy getting "high on life" to be counted on for responsibilities like attending his nephew's bar mitzvah or driving his grandfather to a doctor's appointment. Straying from the traditional parameters of most boy birds, he feels no need to exert a macho aura and has zero compunction about using a loofah in the shower or skipping down the street with his six-year-old niece.

MATING HABITS: His courtship rituals are anything but normal, and while you may not welcome his advances, neither can you ignore them. A Flamingo's approach may be innocently avant garde (offering you a bunch of broccoli in lieu of a bouquet of flowers) or ridiculously uncalled-for (having the waitress send you three piña coladas at one time—all laden with paper umbrellas and pineapple wedges). The uber-confident Flamingo isn't flummoxed by rejection, a familiar scenario for many considering their sexual preference is anyone's guess.

HABITAT: With a natural joie de vivre, he's a real people person and loves crowded places where "enjoying oneself" is the main event, including parades, the Vegas strip, amusement parks (where he may be sidelining as a mime), or concerts (the only guy dancing at a subdued Norah Jones performance).

NEST: A Flamingo forgoes the standard urban professional nest in favor of décor that more aptly echoes his personality. Look for beanbag furniture, inflatable plastic sofas, fiberglass chairs formed to resemble a hand, and accessories like lava lamps or technicolored shag rugs.

HOW TO LURE: Not looking to date a classic beauty or a mousy wallflower, a Flamingo is attracted to girls with a Bedlam-worthy style of their own. Wear bright colors, quirky jester hats, daisies in your hair, or body glitter. Better yet, adopt Annie-Hall man-garb or a Björk swan getup and he'll be instantly intrigued by your kookiness.

FLIGHT PATTERN: He'll dump you in a strange and unique way you never thought possible, like drawing a broken heart on an Etch-a-Sketch or conveying his

> **The Bird, the Boy**
>
> Flamingo birds preen their feathers using oil that's excreted from a gland at the base of their tail. In the same way, Flamingo boys have no aversion to beauty products like hair gel, tanning oil, greasepaint, pancake makeup, and, in some cases, eyeliner.

thoughts through a game of charades: "Three words! Sounds like: 'Eye . . . Knead . . . Space?' "

PRIZED FOR: Generally managing to "turn your frowns upside down," whether that involves leading you by the hand to splash in a city fountain *Friends*-style or driving you on his Vespa to go buy the fixin's for s'mores.

The Subspecies

Lord of the Whimsy
(Circus maximus)

With bright sparkling eyes and a face full of sunshine, Lord of the Whimsy will perchance drive a VW bug, will liberally use emoticons in e-mail text, and is the only guy at the office with a troll pencil topper. His nicknames for you include "Munjee" and "Fuzziboonwinkles," and he can build you a working waffle iron out of Legos.

BOY TIP: Impress him by turning a cartwheel on the sidewalk or quoting a line from *Willy Wonka and the Chocolate Factory*. (A good one to try: "A little nonsense now and then is relished by the wisest men.")

CHARACTERISTIC SONG: Calliope music; "Puff the Magic Dragon" by Peter, Paul & Mary.

Señor Strobe Light
(Discotequius oblivious)

Just as flamingo birds pefer a warm climate, Señor Strobe Light thrives in locales like Cancún, Miami Beach, or on cruise ships (where he's often seen leading conga lines or the Limbo). He loves club-hopping at cheesy nightclub/restaurant establishments named "Rain" or "Bliss," and shelling out $15 and up for a pistachio-flavored martini. During the day, look for him on the beach (tanning salons on cloudy days) soaking up the sun in a neon green thong bathing suit. He occasionally carries a man-bag.

BOY TIP: Since he's attracted to bright, shiny objects, try wearing clothing with plenty of sequins and rhinestones. Stick to styles that reveal your figure. If you shake your bootie in this sort of apparel, five minutes later, he'll be whispering in your ear and licking your neck.

CHARACTERISTIC SONG: "Copacabana" by Barry Manilow.

The Thespian
(Dramaticus personae)

Forever drawn to the spotlight, the Thespian practices "the craft," summoning up raw emotion in acting class by roaring like a lion or wilting like a flower to get in touch with his primal feelings. At auditions, he may change his name from Jim Smith to "Finn Patrick Hoffman," since having three names signifies talent. Playing a clump of grapes in a Fruit of the Loom commercial is his one and only claim to fame.

Research Tools

Mork from Ork

*

Eddie Izzard

*

Andy Warhol

*

Saturday Night Live's
Mango

*

Ziggy Stardust

BOY TIP: Get used to his bizarre behavior and method acting: One day he'll walk around the house squishing and contorting his facial muscles as he repeats "A-E-I-O-oooo." The next, he'll pretend to be a Polish immigrant circa 1902, complete with inaccurate dialect.

CHARACTERISTIC SONG: The old standards, "On Broadway," "Hooray for Hollywood," and "There's No Business Like Show Business."

✳

Flamingos
and the Women Who Love Them . . .

Got a thing for Flamingos? It means you don't view the world in bland black and white. Color, capriciousness, and a bit of drama is what you crave, and Flamingos will deliver that in spades. Your zest for life has led you to seek out society's most eccentric specimens, hoping that in return, a Flamingo will fill your world with sunshine, lollipops, rainbows, and everything that's wonderful. Yet all that Flamingo-boy fun isn't without a cost: You might have to endure some gaping-mouthed stares from bewildered passersby who may be taken aback by your man's not-so-pedestrian presentation. Yet it's easy to understand the intrigue offered from a guy who lives a life full of exclamation points and/or metaphorical neon lights. He's the Lucky Charms leprechaun in human form, and his wacky personality may just be your pot of gold.

✳

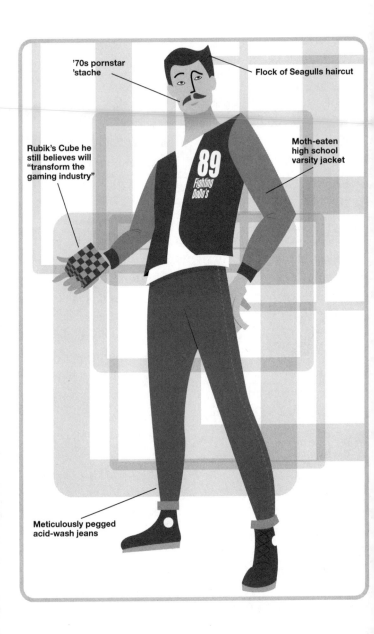

'70s pornstar 'stache

Flock of Seagulls haircut

Rubik's Cube he still believes will "transform the gaming industry"

Moth-eaten high school varsity jacket

89 Fighting DoDo's

Meticulously pegged acid-wash jeans

18

Dodos

They all crowded round her once more, while the Dodo
solemnly presented the thimble, saying "We beg your ac-
ceptance of this elegant thimble"; and, when it had fin-
ished this short speech, they all cheered.

Alice thought the whole thing very absurd . . .

—Lewis Carroll, *Alice in Wonderland*

There's some speculation on whether the dodo
bird got its name from the Dutch word
dodoor, which means sluggard, or the Por-
tuguese word *duodo*, which means foolish and simple. Precise connotations aside, we do know that
while alive, these fat old birds got so comfortable living on a predator-free island that, with a bit of time
and evolution, they lost their need and ability to fly,
becoming take-home Happy Meals for newly ar-
rived colonists and prey. Just as the birds they're
named for have long been extinct, Dodo boys would
rather live in the past than join the pace of the 21st
century. These throwbacks show a dim-witted reluc-
tance to change, stubbornly adhering to beliefs that

have aged more like a carton of milk than a fine cabernet. Suffice it to say, there's no speculation on how the Dodo boy got *his* name.

PLUMAGE: Unable to answer the evolutionary demands of fashion, most Dodos are walking wardrobe "Don'ts," adopting age-inappropriate styles and eschewing today's trends for yesterday's painter's caps, bellbottoms, and light-up LA Gear gym shoes. ("They're hot on the West Coast.") Some may display a disturbing time-warped haircut à la New Kids on the Block, or perhaps even a mullet. Unlike the Hiperati, Dodos do not mean these gestures to be ironic.

BEHAVIOR: Whether it's the family values of the '50s or the musical stylings of the '80s, Dodos are forever nostalgic for a different era. They lament the loss of old fads (*Miami Vice*, big band, and Ronald Reagan) and reminisce about obscure but celebrated moments in their past. ("When Europe sang 'The Final Countdown' for the finale, man, that was hot!") Confused by technology, they hopelessly bungle any attempt to program a VCR and are unable to define TiVo. ("Aren't those water sandals?")

MATING HABITS: Depending on your point of view, Dodos are either proponents of old-fashioned romance or sexist throwbacks, as they insist on holding every door open and always paying. Dates with Dodos will likely consist of a dinner at Denny's, followed by a drive around town and a prompt drop-off at your door by nine, even on Saturday nights. He'll use the phrase "going together" to describe your relationship.

HABITAT: Look for Dodos wearing plaid pants on the local golf course, combing through record stores for used vinyl, hastily scrawling down pencilled notes at retirement planning seminars, leading swing dance classes, driving a mere fifty-four miles an hour on the freeway, or "gone fishin'."

NEST: Most prominent in the Dodo's nest is an over-sized, worn-in recliner, perfect for watching football games, playing Atari, or having an after-dinner brandy. For leisure time, he owns a lifetime sub-scription to *Reader's Digest* and a cassette collection of the Police's greatest hits (purchased via late-night infomercial) to play on his boombox.

HOW TO LURE: To catch his attention, drop obscure ref-erences from another era (Sea Monkeys, *Schoolhouse Rocks,* that commercial with the crying Native American on the side of the road). If he's nervous about technology, tell him you hate that "newfan-gled stuff" and if you had your way, the whole coun-try would still be taking horses and buggies to work.

FLIGHT: Sooner or later, you'll shudder to realize that even though he's not yet your dad's age, your dad is actually cooler than he is. At that point, your rela-tionship will go the way of the real dodo.

The Bird, the Boy

Scientists believe the now-extinct dodo once ate rocks and seeds to serve as digestion aids. Similarly, many a Dodo boy has fanatically sought out food with high fiber content, as being irregular leaves him feeling highly out of sorts.

PRIZED FOR: Dodos are interesting mates for anyone studying cultural anthropology or archaeology, as they're priceless specimens of a period long gone. ("Oh my God! Are those really parachute pants?")

The Subspecies

Old Man Boy
(Rip vanwinkleum)

This seemingly virile young man seems to be channeling the spirit of Bob Hope or George Burns, always complaining about his aches and pains and forever lamenting the forward march of time. Early to bed and early to rise, his day is filled with crossword puzzles, chess games in the park, military histories, lame attempts at humor with neighborhood children ("Where'd my thumb go?"), and dinner at 5 p.m. sharp.

BOY TIP: When watching television with him, expect lengthy and tedious lectures on the evils of modern society: "If it were really 'the real world' they'd be evicted by their landlord by now and thrown out on the street. Kids today are just lazy!"

CHARACTERISTIC SONG: "Old Time Rock-n-Roll" by Bob Seger and the Silver Bullet Band; "My Way" by Frank Sinatra.

Pegs-His-Pants Boy
(Everybody wangchungium)

Unable to grasp that what made Johnny Depp cool in *21 Jump Street* was Johnny Depp, not his hair, Pegs-His-Pants Boy spends hours feathering and spraying his bangs in an elaborate Flock of Seagulls crest. He prefers the work of Marky Mark the singer vs. that of Mark Wahlberg the actor, and wonders why no one else ever kicks back with a wine cooler any more.

BOY TIP: To lure this guy, peg your own pants: (1) With your bottom pants cuff, make a vertical fold (or "peg") one to two inches wide; (2) Pin down the vertical peg with one finger, putting pressure on it to keep the fold straight; (3) Begin to roll up the bottom of your pants in one inch increments, keeping the vertical peg neatly in place with outside pressure until a satisfactory length is reached (usually three to five rolls). Voilá!

CHARACTERISTIC SONG: "Stuck in a Moment" by U2; "If I Could Turn Back Time" by Cher.

Creepy Old Guy
(Scaly loungelizardius)

Unlike Old Man Boy who is young but acts old, Creepy Old Guy is old but acts like a member of the flavor-of-the-moment boy band. What little hair he has left he wears in either a product-enhanced spiky look or a wispy ponytail, accenting it with an earring (because that's "hip and youthful"). Every night of the week, Creepy Old Guy pulls on his leather jacket, whips out his gold pinky ring, hops in his sports car—top down—and goes "clubbing."

Research Tools

Back to the Future (for both the time-travel theme and Michael J. Fox's late '80s sex appeal)

*

Time Machine by H.G. Wells

*

A Connecticut Yankee in King Arthur's Court by Mark Twain

BOY TIP: Be prepared for irritating and obvious statements made in an effort to up his cool ante, like when he states REM is one of the best bands of "our" generation even though his generation listened to the Motown sound.

"Forever Young" by Rod Stewart; "Young Girl Get Out of My Mind" by Gary Puckett and the Union Gap.

The Boomerang Boy
(Proverbial badpennyius)

Whether it's from sheer boredom, a new state of singledom, or the desire that comes from watching birds and bunnies mate during spring, the Boomerang Boy is the ex who inappropriately reappears, ludicrously expecting to pick up where he left off years prior. Unlike other Dodos, whose plumage clearly identifies them as such, this type is identified solely by his retroactive attraction. While your last words to him may have been the sobbing phrase "I hope you rot in hell," three years later, he'll give you a casual call, acting as if

Chicks They Dig
**The Donna Reed
Doyenne**

*

**Shoulder-Pad Wearing
Sheena Easton
Lookalike**

you've always been the best of friends and inquiring about the welfare of your dog and great-aunt (both of whom have since passed away).

BOY TIP: While the Boomerang Boy's instincts are akin to a lost family pet who makes an incredible journey to find its way home after years of separation, you will feel this type's tracking skills to be asinine and pathetic rather than warm and fuzzy.

CHARACTERISTIC SONG: "Keep Coming Back" by Edie Brickell; "I Want You Back" by the Jackson Five.

❄

Dodos
and the Women Who Love Them . . .

While Dodos may seem "so last season" for many women, others see nothing wrong with their reliquary ways. If you've got your eye on a Dodo, you recognize the dependable nature of his unchanging tastes. Perhaps you get a kick out of visiting historic pioneer villages, take pleasure in those radio '70s flashback weekends, or secretly wish you were still in high school. In the great scheme of the universe, time is relative (or so physicists would have us believe), so what difference does it make if a Dodo is holding down the rewind button of life in a subconscious move to avoid his own personal extinction? Once he's latched on to something, he'll hold on steadfast and stubbornly, whether it's those acid-washed jeans, his '78 Gremlin, or you.

❄

Bizarre Bird Fact

The last known dodo bird died in 1681. Yet prompted by eyewitness accounts from two European visitors who reported seeing live dodos on Mauritos, researcher William Gibbon launched an expedition to the island in the 1990s to search for the birds. None were found.

Predatory eyes, clearly on the make

Come-hither smile

Slick business suit, essential gear for his ruthless climb up the corporate ladder

Pocket for stashing his wedding ring

Flashy Rolex

19

Vultures

O Regan, she hath tied
Sharp-toothed unkindness, like a vulture, here.
—William Shakespeare, *King Lear*

What kind of savage God allows a precious baby bunny to become the pick-me-up equivalent of a Snickers bar for some airborne predator on the hunt for fresh meat? Worse still, what cruel and callous deity would create the Vulture boy, who tears through his bevy of nameless babes, leaving only the remains of their bruised and battered hearts? With their imposing good looks, devilish charm, and Machiavellian mystique, Vultures can be hard to resist, making it easy for them to lure unsuspecting beauties into their nest. You, too, may get suckered into thinking you can tame him and reform his "bad boy" ways. We just hope you like soccer, 'cause he's likely to kick your heart around as if it were the ball and he were David Beckham.

PLUMAGE: While some Vultures can be easily detected by their lurid stare, greedy smile, and purposeful swagger, still others go the route of a wolf in sheep's clothing, camouflaging themselves in the guise of an esteemed Eagle or trainable Parakeet. Hot or not, he genuinely believes himself to be a super-fly stone fox and will manage to convince you of the same. Listen to your instincts when trying to identify a Vulture. If you sense an initial "too good to be true" vibe, trust your gut: He is.

BEHAVIOR: From the boardroom to the bedroom, conquest is the Vulture's game as he ruthlessly seizes what he wants, mindless of the carnage left in his wake. Thinly veiled behind a façade of "good ol' boy" charm, he's often hiding a secret life—like, say, his three *other* girlfriends. On his unimpeded climb up the corporate ladder, he'll cheat and backstab the very same male underlings who revere him. The ultimate megalomaniac, he's got a penchant for solving problems with his fists. While his threats are rarely idle, there is often a small chink in the Vulture's armor, be it his irrational fear of going bald, his soft spot for reruns of *The Golden Girls,* or the crippling intimidation he feels in the presence of his own mother.

MATING HABITS: Spotting his prey, he'll circle in on you (cue *Jaws* music), attempting to literally charm your pants off with his urbane wit and magnetic sex appeal. He'll treat you to dinner at a pricey restaurant, hoping you'll feel obligated to "repay him" at the end of the date. Should he score, chances are the Vulture will abscond from your bed in the middle of the night. On the other hand, he may not release his talons so readily, instead displaying possessive tendencies when you try to end things. An eager scavenger, the Vulture scouts out young, wounded women who have already had their hopes crushed by other men, making it all the more easy for him to feed off the scraps of their ravaged hearts.

HABITAT: The Vulture feels most at home in dark bars, where inebriated nymphets are more prone to his advances. In daylight hours, he'll perch at the mostly male corporate offices of a cutthroat, high-stakes brokerage or international banking firm.

NEST: Just as the turkey vulture hisses and groans when his nest is disturbed, don't try snooping around a Vulture boy's stuff, as it could expose his lonely and vulnerable inner core—or the hidden camera he's got set up in his bedroom closet.

HOW TO LURE: Don't. Period.

FLIGHT PATTERN: Once he's killed all your belief in the innate goodness of fellow human beings and destroyed your ability to trust, he'll move on to his next victim. Either that, or he may be obligated to obey your restraining order against him.

PRIZED FOR: Fueling your rage and anger, which in turn prompts you to create great works of art, à la jilted French sculptor Camille Claudel or disco queen Gloria "I Will Survive" Gaynor.

The Subspecies

The Pouncer
(*Instinctivus drawerdropperum*)

While he may be a polite and demure Dr. Jekyll on the first half of your date, a groping, grasping Mr. Hyde emerges once he's got you alone in the passenger seat of his car or camped out on a sofa. With "Russian hands and Roman fingers," the Pouncer's kisses are fast, furious, and as sloppy as a Manwich meal.

BOY TIP: If you invite him into your apartment, be careful not to leave him alone, even momentarily, lest you return to find him waiting for you *sans* clothing.

CHARACTERISTIC SONG: "A Little Less Conversation, a Little More Action" by Elvis Presley; "I Want Your Sex" by George Michael.

He's All Boy
(Testosterum budweisum)

A fan of paging through nudie magazines and listening to Howard Stern, He's All Boy is often found at strip joints and raucous bachelor parties. Just as a vulture bird can pick an antelope's bones clean in twenty minutes, He's All Boy can ingest a plate of buffalo wings with the same rapidity. Has zero proclivity for "metrosexual" activities like using moisturizer or preparing bruschetta. Changes the TV channel whenever a tampon commercial comes on.

BOY TIP: He's All Boy may fool you into thinking he's just a harmless Neanderthal, but after several weeks of entertaining his none-too-romantic booty calls, you'll realize you're nothing more than a carnal convenience.

CHARACTERISTIC SONG: "Mannish Boy" by Muddy Waters; "It's a Man's World" by James Brown; "A Guy Is a Guy" by Doris Day.

The Corporate Climber
(Payrollum assholum)

This predatorial "professional" betrays his colleagues and takes credit for their work but still manages to win the esteem of his boss, who can't see beyond his record-breaking sales numbers (which he often racks up through bribery or subtle intimidation). He'll sleep his way through the office interns, discarding them once he beds them. Look for the Corporate Climber snickering in the back of the room during those obligatory sexual harassment seminars.

BOY TIP: Don't expect the Corporate Climber to settle down with you unless your daddy is Donald Trump, in which case prepare yourself for some Grade A asskissing.

CHARACTERISTIC SONG: "BackStabber" by Eminem; "Barracuda" by Heart.

Secret Agent Man
(Phonium baloneyum)

Imagine a worst-case scenario (a wife and kids; a raging case of genital herpes; a criminal record) and it's probably in his past—or present. If you *only* have his cell phone number, have never seen his place, haven't met his friends, and don't know much about his job (which conveniently involves lots of last-minute "business trips"), first rule out the slight but ever-so-sexy possibility he's in the CIA. Then consider yourself punk'd—and not in that fun, Ashton Kutcher, "Ha-ha! Got me!" sense.

BOY TIP: When you query him on any of his suspicious behavior, expect vague answers followed by attention-distracting flattery. ("Where'd I disappear to last night? Where'd *your hips* disappear to in those jeans? Baby, you look hot!")

CHARACTERISTIC SONG: "Tell Me Lies" by Fleetwood Mac; "Unbelievable" by EMF.

✳

Vultures
and the Women Who Love Them . . .

So you like to flirt with danger and dance with the devil, huh? Well, Vultures can certainly oblige. If you secretly dug the hot jerk who beat up Ralph Macchio in *The Karate Kid*, it's safe to say you harbor an interest in this malicious breed. Whether you're easily intimidated or tough enough to take whatever he dishes out, don't be surprised if a Vulture tears through your life like a tornado. You may consider yourself up to the task of taming this wild one, and turning him into a one-woman kind of guy. Well, go for it, sister. Just remember: Those who do not learn from Tori Spelling's TV movie *Mother May I Sleep with Danger?* are doomed to repeat it.

✳

20

Eagles

Avoid the reeking herd,
Shun the polluted flock,
Live like that stoic bird
The eagle of the rock.
—Elinor Hoyt Wylie, "The Eagle and the Mole"

When thou seest an eagle, thou seest a portion of genius;
lift up thy head!
—Wiliam Blake, *The Marriage of Heaven and Hell*

It's been called a lion of the sky. In ancient times, it was thought to be a messenger from the gods or an omen for the birth of a great king. Today, it's our national bird, and its noble visage can be found on currency next to giant, floating presidential heads. The eagle is symbolic of what our nation aspires to be: powerful, respected, and strong. Similarly, the Eagle boy is symbolic of what a nation of women aspire to date: a man who's kind without being a wuss, strong without being a show-off, clever without being pretentious, unique without being a freak. If he's rich, he's not showy. If he's poor, he's not grungy. An Eagle boy is, as Goldilocks put it, "just right."

PLUMAGE: The Eagle stands confident, with excellent posture and strong features that seem to speak volumes about his inner strength and spirit. Like Plato's notion of the forms, he can come in many shapes and sizes, but for whatever reason, he'll fix your idea of perfection: a bald head you want to kiss or a thick shock of curls you want to run your fingers through; a gorgeously flawless smile or crooked teeth you find charming; a strong preference for boxers or a predilection for briefs.

BEHAVIOR: The Eagle is a walking commercial for the best of mankind: He volunteers at homeless shelters, loves walking his dog or curling up with his cat and a book, and always does dishes for his mom after family meals. Gentlemanly and charming, he urbanely handles every situation he encounters, from gracefully tackling a villain who absconded with an old woman's purse to rationally talking a small child out of throwing a public temper tantrum.

MATING HABITS: Much like the real-life golden eagle returns to the same nesting site year after year, the Eagle boy is faithful, loving you and only you. He'll bring you tasteful bouquets—understated lilies or graceful tulips, never dyed-blue carnations. The unspoken chemistry you share upon first meeting is equally intense, as if the two of you are both silently acknowledging that you will eventually be ripping each other's clothes off at some future date. You may feel slightly (or extremely) intimidated by him and his perfection, but this is your own doing as he does nothing to make you feel in any way inferior and is forever complimenting and praising you.

HABITAT: A favorite among women who are hunting for mates, Eagle boys are, sadly, just as endangered as their feathered friends. When they do appear, they're quickly snatched up for their future role as one half of a long-term committed relationship. You can, however, rule out a few places where they *won't* be: XXX movie theaters, prison, and white supremacist gatherings.

NEST: Upon entering, you may feel as if you're hallucinating, bowled over by this mystical land of cleanliness and taste. Rest assured: His nest really *is* this perfect—originally decorated with nary a piece of chain-store furniture in sight; spotlessly clean, but not museum pristine (except in the bathroom, where it counts most); a fridge full of bright fruit and vegetables; a fresh supply of coffee beans (vs. the freeze-dried variety); a clean bowl of water for his cat; an extra toothbrush he bought for you.

HOW TO LURE: While many well-intentioned friends may tell you it'll happen when you're not looking for it, disregard this clichéd and unhelpful advice. (When *aren't* you looking for it?) Instead, pray mightily to God, Allah, the Mother Goddess, Zeus,

The Bird, The Boy

Known for their graceful courtship displays, Eagles mate by locking talons in the sky and cartwheeling down, beating their wings slowly to ease the fall. Such displays take place each breeding season, even if the birds have been mates for years. Similarly, an Eagle boy is a creative gymnast in bed, and maintains this artistic vigor even when you've been with him longer than you can remember being without him.

and any other deity you may give credence to, then try to place yourself in the intersection of optimum astrological alignment and fate so that due to a series of extreme romantic-comedy-esque coincidences, he magically appears. ("On my flight to Phoenix, I started choking on a peanut, and he rushed down the aisle to give me the Heimlich! We've been together ever since.")

FLIGHT PATTERN: Once Eagles have found a mate, they don't leave. It's true love. If you find him having secret talks with a female coworker, don't worry: It's only to determine the size of your ring finger so he can resize his great-grandmother's antique engagement ring. The only reason an Eagle will leave is to give you the time *you* need. If for any reason you do break up, it won't be the result of some asshole thing he did, like sleep with a hooker and give you a VD. It will be a much more respectable and adult break-up.

("Honey, I feel like you can't become the ballerina you need to be if I keep taking up your time. Go, darling, and live your dreams!")

PRIZED FOR: Restoring your faith in the mating process and making you want to weed through all the other men out there in the hopes that you will one day meet, then wed and/or bed an Eagle. He'll see you as the beautiful, smart, and wonderful person you are.

The Subspecies

Upwardly Mobile the Third
(Gracious richyrichius)

Upwardly Mobile the Third comes from a dynastic breed of wealth and beauty, like the Kennedys, Rockefellers, or Guggenheims. Bred for a life of luxury, he still chooses his own destiny, opting to start out his career with time in the Peace Corps or teaching special education. Once he does elect to follow the family path, he will bring the company to new heights of profitability while creating the highest employee retention rate in its history, often jumping in to work hands-on with his employees. The only thing he lavishes money on is you, and even that's tasteful and nonostentatious.

BOY TIP: Learn to use the word *summer* as a verb.

CHARACTERISTIC SONG: "Pennies from Heaven" by Bing Crosby.

Captain Hot
(Do-gooder extraordinarius)

Whether he's a firefighter, police officer, doctor, or ambulance driver, Captain Hot spends his days in superhero mode, protecting the weak and defending the helpless. He might have a slight God complex from time to time, but considering he delivers babies or saves the lives of critically ill patients, can you really blame him? Captain Hot's got a build that'll allow him to swoop you up in his arms and carry you away like in the final scene from *An Officer and a Gentleman*. Plus, he's so sweet and disarming he could make Big Bird look like an a-hole.

BOY TIP: You'll be drawn to Captain Hot not only because of his uniform (sexy!) and your childhood crush on *CHiPs*'s Ponch or *E.R.*'s George Clooney, but also because it seems like he can protect you from every evil of the world, be it horrific bosses, red-alert scenarios, or flat tires.

CHARACTERISTIC SONG: "I Need a Hero" by Bonnie Tyler; "Someone Saved My Life Tonight" by Elton John.

Effortlessly Beautiful
(Naturalus masterpieceium)

The most stunning man you've ever met, Effortlessly Beautiful doesn't flaunt his appearance, nor does he even seem aware of his gorgeousness. Not only does he eschew hair product, he can wear hole-ridden jeans and a dirty thermal tee in the middle of a tornado and still look hot. Gifted with a body chemistry that doesn't allow for bad breath or body odor, Effortlessly Beautiful tends to fall for ordinary girls with heart and substance over the stunning model type.

BOY TIP: If you can get past him being prettier than you, he makes for a good mate who will turn you on throughout the years, even when he's adopted the old-man silvery look. (Think Paul Newman.)

CHARACTERISTIC SONG: "Take My Breath Away" by Berlin; "Damn, I Wish I Was Your Lover" by Sophie B. Hawkins.

The Lloyd Dobler
(Romeo nextdoorius)

The Lloyd Dobler is the everyday guy who humbly steps up to the challenge of being Prince Charming and passes with flying colors. Wooing you with simple gestures, he might show up at your door in a rainstorm with a pack of marshmallow Peeps or bring your cat a treat on your first date. He's prone to saying spontaneous lines that melt your heart—when you tell him you think he's too wonderful to be true and you're waiting for the other shoe to drop, he'll respond: "I have no other shoe. I'm a one-legged man." You feel moments like this should be accompanied by the buildup of a powerful, inspiring musical soundtrack like *St. Elmo's Fire*.

BOY TIP: Unemployed, bad fashion or musical taste, or rotten breath—nothing's too much for you to get past because this is the man you love.

CHARACTERISTIC SONG: "The Search Is Over" by Survivor.

Hatchling Behavior

As a child, the young Eagle frequently protected the socially less fortunate, whether pummeling the bully of an underprivileged girl or using the power of his popularity and keen Eagle wit to mock those who teased geeks.

❋

Eagles
and the Women Who Love Them . . .

So you've got yourself an Eagle? What can we say? You're a lucky, lucky girl. Perhaps you should start playing the lottery, because the Fates all seem to be lined up in your favor. With an Eagle by your side, your future will surely mimic all the fairy-tale forecasts of happily ever after. Remember, though, there are legions of women out there still desperately seeking this end-all and be-all of manly perfection, and you should graciously share your riches of fortune: Offer to set your sister up with his kind cousin, never give phony, smug-married advice ("I miss being single!"), and enjoy your relationship without flaunting it. After all, you've put in countless hours of boywatching in the wild dating kingdom and have managed to nab this most sought-after national treasure. So much for bad dates that prompt you to murmur "Houston, we have a problem." Now that *this* Eagle has landed, it's one small step for womankind—and a giant leap for you.

❋

Quiz

Name That Bird:
Who's Your Feathered Type?

Got your eye on an Eagle? Have a taste for Turkey? Pining away over a Parrot? No matter what kind of chick you are, there's a guy out there who will fit your bill. Take this quiz to find out which boy type best suits your personality. Simply check the box next to every statement that applies to you. When you're done, tally up the numbers for each checked box using the chart provided on page 212. Whichever bird you've marked most often may well be your perfect match!*

❑ 1. I don't mind one-night stands. In fact, sometimes I prefer them. **(6) (8)**

*The authors claim no responsibility for any mates you may choose to pursue as a result of taking this quiz. Don't blame us if your relationship doesn't fly.

❑ **2.** As far as I'm concerned, California is just the apocalypse waiting to happen. **(3)**

❑ **3.** I wouldn't judge a guy (even subconsciously) if he couldn't change a tire. **(13)**

❑ **4.** I love when a guy writes me poetry—even crappy "roses are red" drivel. **(14)(19)**

❑ **5.** I like men with an aura of mystery to them— they're so very "Johnny Depp." **(20)**

❑ **6.** Iceman in *Top Gun* was one hottie I'd enjoy getting my hands on. **(8)**

❑ **7.** Making out in public is perfectly appropriate for two crazy kids in love. **(19)**

❑ **8.** I'm not fazed by a companion who changes TV channels as frequently as he blinks. **(6)**

❑ **9.** Trying to make small talk with strangers at a party is a fate worse than death. **(20)**

❑ **10.** Guys pay on dates. I won't even attempt the charade of reaching for my wallet when the bill comes. **(15)**

❑ **11.** I have no problem being "the other woman." **(8)**

❑ **12.** I'm willing to go along with someone else's ideas, as long as they keep me interested. **(6)**

❑ **13.** I can hum the theme song to *Masterpiece Theater*. **(11)(14)**

❑ **14.** I reapply my makeup before going to bed with my boyfriend. **(15)**

☐ **15.** I believe there *is* such a thing as an all-out "perfect guy." **(7)**

☐ **16.** When a guy serenades me I get weak in the knees. **(18)(19)**

☐ **17.** The romantic comedy is my favorite film genre because those are movies that give me hope. **(7)(19)**

☐ **18.** I'd subtract two years from my life to date a hot celebrity. **(15)**

☐ **19.** My parents typically approve of the guys I date. **(1)(7)(9)**

☐ **20.** I prefer Brat Pack–partying Charlie Sheen to married-with-baby Charlie Sheen. **(8)**

☐ **21.** I have (or have considered getting) breast implants. **(15)**

☐ **22.** My friends tell me I'm way too picky. **(7)**

☐ **23.** I'd rather ride on the back of a Harley than sit shotgun in a Porsche. **(20)**

☐ **24.** I'm happy to stay home on a Friday night with a good book. **(14)**

☐ **25.** If my perfect guy had an extra finger growing out of his stomach, I'd still think he was perfect. **(7)(17)**

☐ **26.** I buy humorous greeting cards with sarcastic undertones rather than schmaltzy sentimental ones. **(3)**

❑ **27.** In college, I changed my major (or transferred schools) several times before graduating. **(6)**

❑ **28.** I would date a guy who gets manicures. **(15)**

❑ **29.** A man in uniform turns me on—as long as he's not an asshole. **(7)**

❑ **30.** If the guy I love loses his job, files for bankruptcy, and gets a bad case of highly contagious crusted Norwegian scabies, I'd still love him. **(7) (17)**

❑ **31.** While I may to hate to admit it, appearance is a major factor in determining who I date, no matter how nice the potential guy is. **(8) (15)**

❑ **32.** I like cuddling with small puppies and kittens. **(19)**

❑ **33.** I'd rather staple my finger to the wall than hurt someone's feelings. **(2) (9)**

❑ **34.** I'd rather date a good conversation partner than the strong, silent type. **(12)**

❑ **35.** I'd rather date Kramer than Jerry Seinfeld. **(6) (4) (16)**

❑ **36.** Bashful was my favorite dwarf—it's sweet when a guy acts all nervous around me. **(13)**

❑ **37.** I'd take aloof over clingy any day. **(20)**

❑ **38.** I'm a terrific flirt (giggle-wink-smile-blush). **(19)**

❑ **39.** I like sharing my opinions on customer feedback surveys. **(12)**

- [ ] **40.** I'd rather date Ryan than Seth from *The OC*. **(20)**

- [ ] **41.** I hate being cooped up in my house—even on rainy days. **(6)**

- [ ] **42.** I hate even a few seconds of awkward silence on dates. People should always have *something* to say—even if it's just boring chitchat. **(12)**

- [ ] **43.** I prefer James Dean to Owen Wilson. **(20)**

- [ ] **44.** I don't care what people say: Babies look like mini old men and small children are irritating. **(3)**

- [ ] **45.** My ideal vacation involves croissants, street names with "rue," and scooters. **(14)**

- [ ] **46.** I'd like to stay home and rent a movie with my sweetie rather than go out to a club for drinks and dancing. **(9)**

- [ ] **47.** I'd rather hang out with Robin Williams than Tom Cruise. **(6) (16)**

- [ ] **48.** I have requested the "Jennifer Aniston haircut" in my lifetime. **(10)**

- [ ] **49.** I have dated a guy ten years or more my junior. **(11)**

- [ ] **50.** I occasionally watch home decorating shows and the Food Network. **(9)**

- [ ] **51.** I'd date Ernie before I'd date Bert. **(2) (9)**

- [ ] **52.** Nope, Bert's the Muppet for me. **(3) (5)**

❏ **53.** I'd rather tune in to talk radio than listen to music. **(12)**

❏ **54.** Boxing and fistfights are pathetic displays of faux "manliness." **(2)** **(13)**

❏ **55.** Even though I trust him completely, there's no way I'm ever going to allow my guy to go to a bachelor party with strippers. **(9)**

❏ **56.** Problematic bad breath or potent b.o. wouldn't deter me from dating an otherwise great guy. **(17)**

❏ **57.** I enjoy watching *Antiques Roadshow* on PBS. **(11)**

❏ **58.** I have attended the symphony or opera of my own free will at least once in the past three years. **(14)**

❏ **59.** I wish I still dated my high school sweetheart—he was a catch! **(11)**

❏ **60.** I'd rather live in the suburbs than a crowded, busy city—subways and crowds are intimidating. **(9)**

❏ **61.** I'm an excellent listener. **(12)**

❏ **62.** Guys who primp too much are weird and girly. **(17)**

❏ **63.** I'm not settling for anything less than Prince Charming—a guy who'll sweep me off my feet and tell me every morning that I'm more beautiful than the sun. **(19)**

❑ **64.** I'm a total gossip whore—I like to know the dirt on everyone. **(12)**

❑ **65.** I love a five o'clock shadow on a guy. **(17) (20)**

❑ **66.** I admire Bono for his activism as much as his music. **(2)**

❑ **67.** I need a guy who's willing to get down and dirty . . . and by that I mean cleaning the bathroom. **(9)**

❑ **68.** Pee on the toilet seat? No biggie—I grew up with brothers. **(17)**

❑ **69.** In high school, I was a total Marcia Brady, belonging to more than five clubs and organizations. **(6)**

❑ **70.** *Beavis and Butthead* is classic television. **(16) (17)**

❑ **71.** Television eats people's souls. I'd much prefer to read a book. **(14)**

❑ **72.** I read each issue of *Vogue* multiple times. **(10)**

❑ **73.** I'm good and ready to get hot and heavy—quick. **(8)**

❑ **74.** I don't like being the center of attention. **(12)**

❑ **75.** I'd be annoyed if my guy didn't get me flowers or chocolate on Valentine's day. **(19)**

❑ **76.** My legs are typically an unshaved forest—I need a guy who doesn't mind. **(2) (17)**

❏ **77.** If a guy doesn't have a steady, dependable, 9–5 job, I'm not dating him. Why waste my time? **(1)**

❏ **78.** I enjoy reading historical romance novels— guys back then were more romantic than guys today. **(11)**

❏ **79.** On the road of life, it pays to toot your own horn. **(5)**

❏ **80.** I'd love for some Superman to sweep me off my feet. **(7)**

❏ **81.** I'm sorry, but who *doesn't* like a good cup of chamomile tea? **(14)**

❏ **82.** I own a name necklace or a diamond horse-shoe necklace, just like Carrie on *Sex and the City*. **(10)**

❏ **83.** I've sent food back at a restaurant when it wasn't to my liking. **(3)**

❏ **84.** Thrifty guys can walk their cheap ass far away from me—I'd never date one. **(15)**

❏ **85.** I've had dates at T.G.I. Friday's or Chili's. **(1)**

❏ **86.** My MP3 player goes just about everywhere with me. **(18)**

❏ **87.** I hate watching horror and shoot-em-up flicks. **(13)**

❏ **88.** I prefer guys who are wildly gregarious, not shy. **(12)**

❑ **89.** I've seen *Phantom of the Opera*, *Les Mis*, and *Rent*. **(18)**

❑ **90.** A cool car can really start my engine, if you get my drift. **(15)**

❑ **91.** I hate it when old people and little kids cheat at games. **(5)**

❑ **92.** My cell phone bills are astronomical. **(12)**

❑ **93.** I own at least two items from Louis Vuitton, Dolce & Gabbana, or Prada. **(15)**

❑ **94.** I make extensive music mixes for my friends, and I'm pissed if they don't tell me they love a mix within twenty-four hours. **(18)**

❑ **95.** I'll admit it: I dig '80s music like Wham! and Culture Club. **(11)**

❑ **96.** I love adventurous outdoor activities like mountain biking, surfing, or wrestling 'gators. **(6)**

❑ **97.** Fart jokes invariably make me laugh—I just can't help it. **(16)(17)**

❑ **98.** No way would I tool around town in some hand-me-down Chevy. **(15)**

❑ **99.** At a party, the goofball with the lampshade on his head is kind of endearing. **(16)**

❑ **100.** People tell me I fall for guys way too fast. **(19)**

❑ **101.** No cruises or luxury hotel vacations for me— I want to rough it in the natural wild. **(17)**

❑ **102.** With the way things are going now, no way would I want to bring children into this world. **(3)**

❑ **103.** The handsome and talented Harry Connick Jr. holds a prominent place in my heart—and in my CD collection. **(11)(18)**

❑ **104.** I don't mind being the butt of pranks and practical jokes. **(16)**

❑ **105.** On a plane, I'd rather get seated next to Dennis Miller than Mike Meyers. **(3)**

❑ **106.** An occasional feisty spat can really benefit a relationship. Couples who never fight are repressed and passive aggressive. **(5)**

❑ **107.** I have owned something with the words "Von Dutch" strewn brazenly across it. **(10)**

❑ **108.** My life is so stressful that I just need someone to make me laugh. **(16)**

❑ **109.** I love quirky, goofy guys who swim against the stream. **(4)(16)**

❑ **110.** Christopher Walken equals strangely sexy. **(8)**

❑ **111.** People tell me I drive like a geezer. **(11)(13)**

❑ **112.** I'd rather date Will Ferrell than Prince William. **(16)**

❑ **113.** *Willy Wonka and the Chocolate Factory* is one of my favorite movies. **(4)**

❏ 114. I have a subscription to *The New Yorker*. (10) (14)

❏ 115. I'm so tired of guys wanting to jump my bones the minute I meet them—can't we just take our time? (13)

❏ 116. Knock-knock jokes are corny, but they always make me laugh. (16)

❏ 117. I'm a dance-dance-dance-dance-dancing machine. (Watch me get down!) (4) (18)

❏ 118. Cirque de Soleil takes my breath away! (4) (14)

❏ 119. I won't settle for a guy who works a boring 9–5 job. (6) (20)

❏ 120. I have dated a guy ten years or more my senior. (11)

❏ 121. I enjoy skipping, whether it's through a park or down an aisle of cubicles. (4)

❏ 122. I try to play by the rules and not rock the boat. (1) (13)

❏ 123. I shop at The Gap, Limited, and other chain retailers. (1)

❏ 124. I dig rock stars more than actors. (18)

❏ 125. While I'm no Monica Lewinsky, I *am* attracted to guys who are powerful and command respect. (7) (8)

❏ 126. Going to roller rinks is fun! (4) (11)

❏ **127.** I like a guy who isn't afraid to cry. **(13)**

❏ **128.** I wish *Friends* had never ended. **(1)**

❏ **129.** I can't stand people who don't share my musical tastes—if we can't share a favorite band, how can we share the rest of our lives? **(18)**

❏ **130.** I loved Sam and Diane's relationship on *Cheers.* **(5)**

❏ **131.** I hate conflict, and will happily agree to anything just to stop the problem. **(2)(5)**

❏ **132.** I'm looking for a chap like Jane Austen's Mr. Darcy. **(7)(14)(19)**

❏ **133.** I'm looking for someone who's good marriage material, wants to be a dad, and enjoys mowing the lawn. **(1)**

❏ **134.** I love reading *Us Weekly, People,* and fashion mags. **(10)**

❏ **135.** I believe in some conspiracy theories. **(5)**

❏ **136.** I know what "tithing" is and I do it. **(2)**

❏ **137.** My Ugg boots are *really* comfortable, I swear! **(10)**

❏ **138.** When people come to me with their problems, it makes me feel useful. **(3)**

❏ **139.** With his gleaming bald head and devilish grin, Lex Luther is so much sexier than that goody-two-shoes Superman. **(8)**

❏ **140.** I'd like a guy who will take me out to the ballgame. **(1)**

❏ **141.** Tom Hanks is *seriously* irritating. **(3)**

❏ **142.** I know who Steven Cojocaru is. **(10)**

❏ **143.** Shiny, happy people get on my nerves occasionally. **(3) (20)**

❏ **144.** I'm proud to admit I've cast a vote for Ralph Nader. **(2)**

❏ **145.** I'd prefer a guy who's not too flashy or outrageous. **(1) (9)**

❏ **146.** Everybody Loves Raymond—including me. **(1)**

❏ **147.** I liked the White Stripes before they were famous. **(10) (18)**

❏ **148.** My wardrobe (and outlook) resembles Rainbow Brite more than Morticia Adams. **(4)**

❏ **149.** People who eat meat should consider the cows' feelings. **(2)**

❏ **150.** I was on the debate team in high school. **(5) (12)**

❏ **151.** I can kick ass in just about anything I set out to do. **(5)**

❏ **152.** I have grown a trendy mullet, or I've dated someone with a trendy mullet. **(10)**

❏ **153.** I find myself forever drawn to bad boys. **(8) (20)**

❑ **154.** I could never be rude to telemarketers no matter how annoying they are. **(2) (13)**

❑ **155.** Clowns are loveable, not insanely creepy. **(4)**

❑ **156.** I can sometimes be a domineering girlfriend. I usually get my way. **(9) (13)**

❑ **157.** I'm not threatened by a man who wears eyeliner. **(4)**

❑ **158.** Sure, *American Idol*'s Simon crushes dreams, but I appreciate his honesty. **(5)**

❑ **159.** Andrew Lloyd Weber equals Andrew Lloyd *wonderful*! **(18)**

Who's Your Feathered Type?

1	2
3	4
5	6
7	8
9	10